My Only
Friend Is
Darkness

Note to the ICS Reprint Edition

My Only Friend Is Darkness was originally published by Ave Maria Press, Notre Dame, Indiana, 46556, in 1988. We are especially grateful to Frank J. Cunningham of Ave Maria Press for his generous assistance in this reprint edition.

Until recently, ICS Publications has been known primarily for its critically-acclaimed translations of the classics of Carmelite spirituality. Our success in these endeavors now enables us to begin offering popular commentaries in the same field, and reprints of excellent works no longer available elsewhere. From the testimony of its many earlier readers, we trust that the reprint of this volume by Barbara Dent will continue to provide guidance and solace for those undergoing life's "dark" experiences.

My Only Friend Is Darkness

*Living the Night of Faith
With St. John of the Cross*

Barbara Dent

ICS Publications
Institute of Carmelite Studies
Washington, D.C.
1992

V ery special thanks from the author to Mary Freiburger, who has worked so hard and done so much to place my works. I am indebted to her at every level, and publicly affirm my warmest gratitude and high regard. And also to Irene Dromgool, my willing faithful typist of Tuakau, New Zealand.

ICS Publications
2131 Lincoln Road NE
Washington, DC 20002-1199

ACKNOWLEDGMENTS

Some of these chapters have been printed whole, in part, or in altered form in the periodicals *Mt. Carmel* and *Spiritual Life*.

PERMISSIONS

Excerpts from THE JERUSALEM BIBLE, copyright © 1966 by Darton, Longman & Todd, Ltd. and Doubleday & Company, Inc. Used by permission of the publisher.
Excerpts from the documents of the Second Vatican Council are from THE DOCUMENTS OF VATICAN II: With Commentaries and Notes by Catholic, Protestant, and Orthodox Authorities, edited by Walter M. Abbot, SJ. Copyright © 1966 by The America Press. Reprinted by permission of The Crossroad Publishing Company.
Quotations by Jean-Pierre Caussade taken from *On Prayer* (London: Burns & Oates, 1949) and *Self-Abandonment to Divine Providence* (London: Burns & Oates, 1959). Used with permission of the publisher.
Quotations by John of the Cross taken from *The Ascent of Mt. Carmel, Dark Night of the Soul* and *The Living Flame of Love,* translated by E. Allison Peers (London: Burns & Oates, 1953). Used with permission of the publisher.
Excerpts from "East Coker" in FOUR QUARTETS, copyright 1943 by T. S. Eliot and renewed 1971 by Esme Valerie Eliot. Reprinted by permission of Harcourt Brace Jovanovich, Inc. (for U.S.A.), and Faber and Faber Ltd. (elsewhere).

Library of Congress Cataloging-in-Publication Data

Dent, Barbara.
    My only friend is darkness: living the night of faith
with St. John of the Cross / Barbara Dent.
      p. cm.
    Originally published: Notre Dame, Ind. : Ave Maria Press, c1988.
    ISBN: 0-935216-19-7
    1. Spiritual life—Catholic Church. 2. Faith. 3. Purgative way
to perfection. 4. Dent, Barbara. I. Title.
[BX2350.2.D447   1992]   92-40476
248.4'82—dc20   CIP

Contents

You have plunged me into the bottom of the pit,
   into the dark abyss.
Upon me your wrath lies heavy,
   and with all your billows you overwhelm me . . .
Companion and neighbour you have taken away from me:
   my only friend is darkness
                              (Ps 87, Confraternity Version).

Just as all men die in Adam, so all men will be brought to life in Christ (1 Cor 15:23).

Unless a grain of wheat falls on the ground and dies,
it remains only a single grain;
   but if it dies
it yields a rich harvest.
Anyone who loves his life loses it;
anyone who hates his life in this world
will keep it for eternal life.
If a man serves me, he must follow me,
wherever I am, my servant will be here too.
If anyone serves me, my father will honor him
                              (Jn 12:24-26).

Thus it is evident to everyone that all the faithful of Christ of whatever rank or status are called to the fullness of the Christian life and to the perfection of charity. By this holiness a more human way of life is promoted even in this earthly society. In order that the faithful may reach this perfection, they must use their strength according as they have received it, as a gift from Christ. In this way they can follow in His footsteps and mold themselves in His image, seeking the will of the Father in all things, devoting themselves with all their being to the glory of God and the service of their neighbor. In this way too, the holiness of the People of God will grow into an abundant harvest of good, as is brilliantly proved by the lives of so many saints in Church history (*Dogmatic Constitution on the Church*, 40).

1 Lighthouse

THE IMMEDIACY OF actual experience brings theological abstracts to
pulsating life.

And so I shall lead into my commentary on the Dark Night by
quoting a personal account of a trial of faith endured many years
ago now, and written down at the time. This kind of trial was for
me an almost constant state, in varying degrees of intensity, for 13
years.

Then came an immediate and complete change into a contrary
state of light, joy and blessedness. After 14 years this in turn was
followed in 1983 by another unexpected jerk which precipitated me
into more than four years of a variation of the "lighthouse experience," only at a much deeper level, with some different emphases
and new elements, and at terrifying intensity.

I have now emerged once more into tranquillity and rest, much
more profound than any I knew before.

This book is concerned with what I learned experientially and
from reading the works of various fellow travellers, especially John
of the Cross, during the two periods when the grain of wheat fell
into the ground and died. Then my only friend was darkness—the
darkness of faith that would not give up affirming what it
believed—yet in that darkness wonders of grace happened.

The record of the "lighthouse experience" was written in the
form of a letter to a very intimate, lifelong friend not unfamiliar
with its perils.

Dear Kathleen,

I'm going to try to reveal to myself and you the existential
situation—exactly how I am and feel in the here-and-now. I'm
about to make myself the illustration of my theme not in any spirit
of detachment, I might stress, but out of a sense of desperation.

Yet, as soon as I say that I know I must qualify it.

It's curious, but the life of creative suffering leads to both integration and disintegration. The integration is when Christ becomes the focal point for all things; the disintegration happens when you become aware that you are operating on several different levels at once.

For example, I speak of a sense of desperation, yet it's true that this doesn't involve my whole being. Even in the midst of desolation and distress I am aware that another part of me goes on quietly believing and trusting. It must, because if it didn't I'd cut my throat; I *feel* despair, and yet I am not in despair.

I become conscious of the separation of will from thoughts and feelings, and within the will a further split between what might be called the self-directed will and the God-directed will, which I'll shorten for convenience to the I-will and the Thou-will.

Anyway, I am going to try to externalize what is in me right now, both by way of illustration of what we were discussing recently, and also because it amounts to an affirmation of faith, something I am badly in need of at present. "I believe: help thou my unbelief," I keep praying.

I suppose, with my lifelong tendency to depression and emotional turmoil, interior states like this are to be expected. How is what I'm now enduring different from what I went through in the years before I had faith?

Well, my despair then was true despair. Often enough I wanted to die, and several times I think I might have attempted to take my own life had not either the fear of physical pain and the general messiness of the procedure or else a kind of residual stoicism prevented me. Certainly I felt my life, and all life, had no purpose, and I was desolately lost in self-hatred and self-contempt coupled with the anguished feeling of being unloved and unwanted by everyone.

Much of my despair arose from a profound sense of defeat. I had longed so much and tried so hard to be "good," only to find I was selfish, sulky, egotistical, proud and eaten up with the longing to be a success and recognized as such. I experienced myself as accursed, belonging nowhere, without destination and meaning. This was psychological, not theological despair. I knew no theology, belonged to no church, considered I had put Christianity behind me as a beautiful but untrue fable. The core of my accursedness was not in any sense of being cast off by God and so destined for hell—the only hell I knew and believed in was in the mind, and here I was right in it. No, the core was in my mother's rejection of me and her actual curse uttered at me, years before.

My state varied between a gray listlessness and an anguish so terrible that I feared insanity. My view of life was an unalleviatedly tragic one.

And how is it different now?

It's important for me to make this clear, because getting it straight in my mind, as I have to do all over again from time to time, helps me to affirm my faith and revitalize my hope.

When I feel despair now, as I have for the last two months or so, how is it different?

In the first place, it's never total despair. Whatever my feelings are, my will never agrees with them. It seems as if it can't, as if it's gripped in a vice and can't move, no matter what the turmoil all about it. Also, whatever the chaotic nature of my thoughts, and however they conform to the old patterns once so painfully habitual, part of my mind knows quite clearly that this is all nonsense.

The reason part is like a lighthouse in a fierce storm. Its light is obscured by waves, clouds and lashing rain, but it's shining all the same, and every now and then a beam lights up the chaos, and when the storm dies down there it is, unmoved, constant, serene. Maybe I could say the will is this lighthouse, the reason is the light in it and the storm is the destructive confusion of despairing emotions and thoughts that get out of control.

Before, there was no lighthouse. The lighthouse is the repository of my faith. And before, there was no faith.

There are times when I feel the lighthouse is gone, overwhelmed and battered out of existence, yet I know it's still there by the fact that I continue to believe, and that I never even consider for a moment taking my own life, or that I'm going mad.

Yes, as I consider it all, I see how very different my life of faith is from my previous existence, and how my view has changed from the tragic to the tragi-comic, with plenty of irony attached to it.

What is it that I continue to believe, no matter what?

Well, with a psychological history that had as its hallmark the suffering of feeling rejected and despised, it's no wonder that during these storms a great deal of my suffering arises from experiencing myself as rejected by God. At least for the last two months, and at other times, it takes the form of feeling God is my enemy, that he deliberately sets out to thwart and deny me, that he spurns me, that he mocks and despises me, that he grinds me under his heel as if I were a slug. (The psalmist often felt this too.)

Yet this is not what I *believe*. If someone said to me, "Your Christian God is a cruel God. He hates you and wants to destroy you," my whole being would respond with the outraged affirmation, "That's a lie!" And yet, this is exactly what I feel, and even what the thoughts in my head are saying. But before I had faith these feelings and these thoughts were all I had. I was completely at their mercy. Now, this is not so.

Which brings me to something else.

At those times earlier in my life I often had a strong sense of an evil presence, of a malignant being that willed my downfall—my madness or my suicide—and was trying to provoke it by aggravating all this despair within me. I use to tell myself that even if I didn't believe in the Christian God, I believed in the devil, for the reality of this Evil One seemed indisputable to me.

I believe I had a true spiritual insight. It was a devil who was actively working to make me despair, and later on I gave him a name, and I still name him so: the Devil of Negativity. Now he is opposed by the Angel of Affirmation who also lives in the lighthouse, but then I was unaware of any angel.

This Devil of Negativity is especially attracted to me, as he is to all those with a tendency to depression and pessimism. He insinuates himself into my thoughts and feelings before I realize it, and he can certainly create misery and confusion. He gets me thinking I'm a failure at everything, that everyone considers me an inferior being. He delights in exaggerated generalities—that my life is purposeless, that it's pointless throwing myself into my work the way I do, that no one wants what I have to give, that all my efforts at anything are useless—and, of course, the trump card, that God is my enemy. Note how cleverly he concentrates my attention upon myself in a kind of tightening spring of fascinated egotism!

Once he gets his toe in he's likely to gain a lot of ground before I do much to help myself, because the tracks are well-trodden from the years of misery before I had faith. It's a bit like a set of chain reactions—one nucleus of thoughts and feelings sets off the next, and before I know where I am, or where he is, I'm in the midst of a hellish din and chaos. And it's hard to get out of. I know—I've been here for what seem interminable weeks now.

Yet it's so simple really.

I remember when I was ill some years ago, and depressed and worried because I didn't know how I was going to get well enough to earn my living again, and also because of the same old thoughts and feelings detailed here, my kind young doctor sat on my bed, encouraged me to talk, and listened sympathetically to my wail of misery. Then he said, "What do you *want* from life?"

It was curious (though to be expected, because it was the simple truth on which I had based my life systematically for years before this event) but in a flash everything in me became calm, lucid, ordered and at peace. I replied, "God's will," and I knew it was so, and because it was so, I need not worry or distress myself over anything. It must be God's will for me to be ill and helpless, and if it was his will I only had to accept it and trust him to bring out of it, in his own way and time, the good that he wanted for me.

The shift from anguish, confusion and fear to peace, order and trust was dramatic and immediate, and I was released, for that particular period, from the unwelcome attentions of the Devil of Negativity.

Before I had faith, I could never have said that. That is one supremely important difference between then and now.

Another equally important factor is my conviction of the all-pervasiveness of Divine Providence. I can't despair, for even while I feel and think despair, I know Divine Providence is in control. For example, it is the series of flattening disappointments and negations of effort over the last few months that has left me feeling listless and defeated now. I truly don't know what to do or where to turn, speaking from a practical point of view, as well as from a spiritual one. When I stop to think, I realize that this means that I don't know what God wants of me. Every time I think I know, and throw myself into something, it ends in defeat. (Or is that only what the Devil of Negativity is telling me? It sounds like one of his half-truths.)

I have felt bewildered, exactly as if a dear friend I loved, trusted, confided in and relied on had not only let me down on every front but publicly spurned me in the bargain. The Devil of Negativity has been capitalizing on this, provoking bouts of rebellion, bitterness, resentment, and general, unclean sourness. I've been fairly helpless. I've even felt I was in a dangerous state spiritually—that I might do something dramatic like "throw everything up" or "go off the deep end."

But now when I sit down to write about it to you, Kathleen, and make the necessary effort to examine it all detachedly, I see how much of it has been false imagination. I felt so desolate (note how often feelings come into this) that I told myself I'd lost the sense of Divine Providence surrounding and supporting me that has been my strength all these years since God gave me faith. Now, as I write, I see that though it was true that I couldn't feel or sense God's providence, I never in fact ceased to believe in its reality and to know that it was there.

"Underneath are the everlasting arms." Instead of feeling their support, I've had the giddying sense of being in a vacuum, and a hostile one at that, but the lighthouse was still there. I was so absorbed in the dramas my false imagination (so cleverly inspired by the Devil of Negativity) was presenting to me, that I forgot to look for its beams. But they were there. Now, in the detachment that comes to me as I write, searching for the truth, I know it. I've been tempted against faith, but all the time my faith's been safe in God's care, strengthened by him, calmly beaming behind all the nightmare darkness of the storm.

And so Divine Providence still had me in its care. However I *felt*, God was in control. It's true he's permitted me to undergo a series of disappointments and defeats to do with my work and my personal life, but he has a plan. I don't know that plan, and with my limited view and, yes, I must face it, egotistical, vain, self-seeking desires, it seems to me that God has senselessly heaved an enormous wrench into my laboriously constructed works. Well, what if he has? He knows what he's doing; the works belong to him, not to me. He can do what he likes with them.

He knows what he's doing. I don't have to know. All I have to do is accept and love and be at peace.

How often I've had to struggle through to this realization! In the end, I always get there—by his grace. This is what I *believe*. Because I believe it, and my belief remains unshaken, even while I *feel* it has been annihilated, my despair is different from that former despair when I had no faith.

God knows best. His Divine Providence is the expression throughout his creation of his infinite love. By means of it he manipulates the catastrophic results of the misuse of free will so that he can bring about a final cosmic good. My sufferings, thwartings, failures, bewilderments, mistakes, and all the rest are woven into the pattern. From my worm's eye view the pattern may seem a senseless muddle; from God's it has a magnificent design and purpose.

He knows. He loves. He is at work. Therefore I can trust him. I can abandon myself to his Divine Providence, which in this instance has expressed itself by a series of apparent negations of my efforts and aims—ones I have genuinely believed were God's will for me. Therefore all this outcry, despair and feeling of failure is senseless. Divine Providence can never fail. If I am abandoned to Divine Providence, one with it, willing what it wills, I can never fail no matter how dismally unsuccessful I may appear to myself and by worldly standards.

Cling to this truth. I believe it. This is a central part of my faith, and it's this that makes sense of the senseless and gives purpose to the purposeless.

I seem to have talked myself back to sanity. If you knew the misery I've been in for nearly three months now! You do know some of it and have responded with your usual warm and loving sympathy, but you couldn't really heal me. This is something I have to do each time myself, by struggling back to the lighthouse, by exercising my faith, by reclaiming my peace.

The result is that I know I have to go on. God has closed doors I thought he was opening for me. Well, I must accept. I've been making a fuss because I didn't get what I wanted. But how do I know it would have been good for me? I have to have such supreme trust in Divine Providence that as soon as it appears to contradict itself I say immediately, "Yes, all right. I want that now, if it's what you want. And I don't want any longer what I thought you wanted for me 10 seconds ago." Always it has to be the Thou-will triumphant over the I-will. I have to get so pliable that I change into fullspeed-reverse from fullspeed-ahead at a moment's notice. I certainly need to put in a lot of practice!

Well, I suppose if I can't learn anything else, at least I can learn that I've a lot to learn yet. I'm a long way from the ideal. St. Francis de Sales expresses it this way: "But a still higher thing is a simple waiting on God's will, for it willingly awaits and accepts a will which has not yet been revealed. It brings one to peace and tranquillity beforehand in all that God may will, no matter how secret and hidden it may be to one."

Yes, that reminds me of the recipe I've often used for myself—to accept *before it happens* whatever God is sending me. I've slipped up on it this time, but at least I do know what to do. In the years before I had faith, I didn't know what to do, and there's the difference—knowing what to do with one's suffering.

And so I accept these humiliations and these defeats. I acknowledge that they are the very best possible thing that could happen to me, however I feel about it. I know that this must be so because Divine Providence has ordained them for me. Because I have given my life to God without reservation, I must agree with the way he runs it. To invite divine intervention into one's life is necessarily to invite what is beyond human understanding. It's no use trying to understand. I am not meant to understand, but to accept in faith and to be at peace.

That peace resides in the will, in the lighthouse in the storm, and it remains there, unperturbed and serene, though all feeling of peace is annihilated by the fury of the tempest outside. It must remain so as long as my will is willing God's will, and they are united in the Thou-will. The will that is the lighthouse is a Thou-will. It is the ephemeral I-will that is involved in the storm outside, being tossed this way and that, torn to shreds, submerged and agonized. The Thou-will is safe in God's will, and nothing in time or in eternity can harm it. Because the seat of the spiritual life is the will, this means that nothing in time or in eternity can harm the essential I, for it is one with God.

In the light of these truths how substanceless all the sufferings of these past weeks appear! I've let myself become immersed in trivialities, and lost (in feeling, not reality) my peace by letting myself fret for what God has shown me was not, after all, his will for me. I clung when he said to let go. I kept going when he changed direction. I couldn't relinquish my human judgment of what was best for me when Divine Providence indicated that divine wisdom had a different view of the matter.

I've suffered for it. The Devil of Negativity has had an orgy and grown bloated on my blood. But he's going to get lean again now. Though I still feel depleted and shaky after his cannibalistic attacks on me, I've separated myself from him again. It's when I identify with him, when I let him take over my I-will, that my state becomes dangerous.

"So stand your ground . . . always carrying the shield of faith so that you can use it to put out the burning arrows of the evil one. And then you must accept salvation from God to be your helmet and receive the word of God from the Spirit to use as a sword.

"Pray all the time, asking for what you need, praying in the Spirit on every possible occasion. Never get tired of staying awake to pray for all the saints" (Eph 6:14, 16-18).

St. Paul uses the metaphor of battle where I use that of storm and lighthouse, but we mean the same thing. It is faith that enables one to conquer, and this faith is a gift from God. Whatever the darkness and the turmoil, faith can still make its affirmations, and as long as it does that, the will is at peace and the spirit whole, though the mind be in confusion and the emotions in torment.

And so, Kathleen, I learn once more, and experience, that God's peace, the peace he gives, passes all understanding, and if sought can be attained.

The Five Lights of Piha

Five lights in the darkness far below,
two to one side, and three in a row . . .

During my insomniac nights
whatever time I awaken, there they are.
Through the uncurtained windows
and the latticed macrocapa boughs
that toss and moan in the winter gales,
tumult everywhere, my hilltop home a fort
the fury of the storm claws at and flails,
those five lights beam, Pompeii soldiers
steadfast, resolute, though chaos looms.

Tonight at three, hours before dawn comes,
I lie awake while the wind screams
to hurricane pitch and the huge boughs lash
at the starless sky. The clamor and crash
jangle my nerves. Vibrations quiver
up through my bed as the wind whips hit
walls and windows like shot. I wonder
how frail glass can hold, and sit
upright against my pillows, eyes
on the rain-lashed space, afraid
the roof will take wing, the walls be razed.
Then through the demented darkness far below
I see five lights.
                    I do not live
on some unpeopled outpost of the universe. This storm
will pass as others have.
My roof and walls will hold, I know.

2 The Seed and Its Harvest

JESUS LOVED TO draw parallels between the observed facts of nature and the interior life of humans. His symbols, so simple yet so powerful, have layer upon layer of meaning.

Fundamental to the growth and development of plants is the life cycle of the seed. The central truth applicable to our relationship with the Trinity is that unless the seed falls into the ground and dies, it cannot bear abundant fruit.

It is in connection with his own passion, death and resurrection and our inevitable share in it if we are to be his disciples, that Jesus says,

> "I tell you most solemnly,
> unless a wheat grain falls on the ground and dies,
> it remains only a single grain;
> but if it dies,
> it yields a rich harvest" (Jn 12:24).

Baptism inaugurates us into the life of Christ, and the other sacraments increase that life in us. We are meant to grow daily in this dimension of Christ-union. In the process, many seeds in us have to be relinquished and let fall into the good soil of his love if we are to bear those fruits of his Spirit for which we were made. We have to invite and submit to change. We have to agree to the pain of renouncing one good in order to embrace a higher one. Constantly we have to be dying on one level in order to be reborn and renewed on another.

This transformation is the work of the Spirit itself issuing from the glorified Christ and coming to us as a result of his own death and resurrection. "Unless I go, / the Advocate will not come to you" (Jn 16:7). Just as the Son of Man rose from death, so we too, through

19

submission to the spiritual death and rebirth cycles of inner growth, will be honored by the Father, sanctified by the Spirit and received into glory with the Lord.

In our cycles of dying and rebirth, we become "coheirs with Christ, sharing his sufferings so as to share his glory" (Rom 8:17). We are absorbed into the *shekinah*, becoming part of the divine Presence in the world, though just as the glory of Jesus was hidden within his humanness, except on Tabor, so ours is concealed both from ourselves and others.

The rare exceptions are when the Spirit manifests herself in visible ways to others through certain chosen persons. Such graces are given not for personal exaltation, but so that others may be uplifted spiritually, begin to hunger for what such graces symbolize, and submit to inner death in order to be reborn into the fullness of life in the Lord.

Not all inner deaths result in spiritual growth and becoming a co-heir with Christ. A commitment must be made, in adult awareness and full sincerity, to what our baptismal promises said and implied.

"When we were baptised in Christ Jesus, we were baptised in his death; in other words, when we were baptised we went into the tomb with him and joined him in death, so that as Christ was raised from the dead by the Father's glory, we too might live a new life. . . . When he died, he died once for all to sin, so his life now is life with God; and in that way, you too must consider yourselves to be dead to sin but alive for God in Christ Jesus" (Rom 6:4, 10-11).

The grace of rebirth is given us at baptism, but if this is infant baptism, then supernatural growth in us requires our fully adult consent to and cooperation with it. To die to sin usually means a long, slow process of enlightenments, deliberate choices, setbacks, graces, trials, temptations, sufferings and growing awareness, as we love and respond to the Trinity within.

Full rebirth in Christ has been attained when we do not experience any division or jarring between our inner self and its outward acts and the Trinity present and active in our depths. The two selves flow together, the one fully subject to the other so that we "do always the things that please him" and he "finds no fault" in us. Human weaknesses and imperfections remain till we die, but in our rebirth process grace comes to dominate them to the degree that God turns to good everything we are and do.

Though deliberate sin of any kind is now carefully avoided, we retain our individuality and will seem obviously imperfect to others. Their strictures remind us, often painfully, of our complete dependence upon grace. We have "put on Christ" as a "garment" over our potentially sinning selves. This divine garment enables us to acknowledge that we have been "freed from the slavery of sin, but only to become slaves of righteousness" (Rom 6:18).

Jesus told Nicodemus (Jn 3:1-21) he had to be "born from above" in order to be able "to see the kingdom of God"—which, though it is in us through our baptism, is seldom realized in this life.

Nicodemus, just like most of those who listened to Jesus' symbolic statements, took him literally, and challenged, "Can [a man] go back into his mother's womb and be born again?" Jesus proclaimed, rather than explained, that "what is born of the Spirit is spirit," a mystery whose action human intellect cannot fathom.

Human minds can be darkened and their judgment marred because too often they "prefer darkness to light" and their "deeds are evil." Jesus told Nicodemus that he had come from God as Savior from this darkness and evil. He must be "lifted up" (on the cross) before humankind could be healed, renewed and reborn.

Presumably Nicodemus pondered all these things in his heart and became Spirit-enlightened, for it was he who spoke on behalf of Jesus, demanding a fair trial for him on the night of his arrest, and he who later brought a quantity of spices for his burial.

We can deduce that he went through his own painful death and rebirth process, emerging into the true Light that lightens the whole world spiritually. The womb of the Spirit had received the seed of his old self, found it fertile, and through the power of the Trinity brought it forth to bear fruit in discipleship.

This is the purpose of spiritual death and rebirth—to serve the Lord and his body, the church, by cooperating in his redemptive work for the world. The Lord went before; the servant follows after.

Jesus himself was like us in all things except sin. Since there never had been and never was any sin in him or in his actions, he had no need to die to personal sin in himself, as we have. Instead, he died to and because of the total racial sin to enable us to die to our personal sin and sinfulness.

He was our scapegoat, victim, proxy, the Suffering Servant in whom no fault could be found, yet who bore our iniquities, taking the shame of us all upon himself (see Is 53).

This was the substance of his cross—the sin of humanity. The actual wood was only symbolic of this inner, spiritual, intolerable burden. Each of us placed our personal load upon his shoulders. Each of us can enter into human and spiritual maturity (rebirth) only by recognizing our personal responsibility for a part of his sufferings and death and making a pact with him to help him instead of loading it upon him knowingly or unknowingly, and then leaving him to carry it alone.

"My yoke is easy," he told us. This kind of Eastern yoke is a double one, so he is asking each of us to be harnessed in conjunction with him to the burden of our and the world's sin. Together we can bear that burden, whether of yoke or cross. Whenever he fell on his journey to Calvary, it meant some of us were shirking our responsibilities. Hanging on the cross, he cried out in dereliction, asking his Father why he had abandoned him. At the same time he was also experiencing human rejection of participation in his salvation work.

We are in this with him, and with and for each other. It is impossible to separate ourselves from his work because of the solidarity of the whole human race in him. We have the choice of making our part positive or negative. If positive, we consent to be the grain of wheat that descends into his passion and death with him, in him, in us, only to rise to new life in his resurrection with him.

We testify with St. Paul, "I have been crucified with Christ." The fruit of this death is to be able to add, "And I live now not with my own life but with the life of Christ who lives in me" (Gal 2:20).

This inner state is a "transforming union." It means we have fulfilled our baptismal destiny by becoming completely incorporated into Christ in spiritual rebirth and new life.

If our part is negative, we identify ourselves with those who raged to Pilate to crucify him, who jeered at him, spat upon him, watched in avid, heartless, sensation-seeking curiosity to see if he could work the miracle of coming down by his own power from the cross—or else we are one with the materialistic and merely indifferent who went about their daily business in Jerusalem as if nothing were happening.

Either way we leave all the work and suffering to Jesus and his followers. We have chosen to dissociate ourselves from the situation. In reality, of course, such a dissociation is impossible.

The Savior and the saved, which means the whole human race, are inextricably together in this redemptive act, mysteriously and incarnationally made one, so that whenever the Father looks upon the Son he also sees all of us.

Few people have written as perspicaciously of the spiritual death and rebirth of which the grain's life/death/life cycle is a metaphor as John of the Cross, the 16th-century Carmelite saint and doctor of the church.

I have found his expositions in *The Ascent of Mount Carmel* and *Dark Night of the Soul* immensely enlightening and practical, but they do not make easy reading. I base much of what I say in this book upon his teachings as I have applied them to my personal experience.

Seed and Sun

Subterranean secret caverns where
water channels gush in darkness.
Impenetrable depths of cold clay
walls of earth where blind worms push.
    In these the seed is thrust and dies.

A granule of masked promise lodged
among the slabs of pain's contorted strata
folded and compressed by earthquakes
that heave and rack with shock and wrench.
    Travail synthesizes seed with clod.

Spasmodic throes remold
and sculpt anew the tangled caves
twist streams like helpless string
toss boulders up like pingpong balls
on fountain jets, scribble rock layers.

Chaos and underworld unite
to bury microscopic seed
past resurrection.
                    But then some code
too cryptic for our grasp commands response.
Seed tingles, stirs, alerts itself, recalls
its hieroglyphic destiny
compressed minutely like a pater noster
threepence-cramped.
                    Seed thrusts toward
the liturgy of bird-blithe boughs
and showers slanting in the air and light.

3 And Now It Was Night

In JOHN'S GOSPEL, chapter thirteen, we read of Jesus at supper with his friends on the night he was betrayed. Jesus knew what Judas intended to do and even gave him specific permission to do it.

"What you are going to do, do quickly" (Jn 13:27).

Judas went out on his traitor's errand, and the gospel adds simply and with profound metaphorical meaning: "Night had fallen."

Later Jesus also went out into that actual and symbolic night. What he endured and what happened to him from then until he came, risen and alive, out of the tomb, is where all those who pass through their individual dark nights find purpose, meaning, hope and the power to cling on.

The term *dark night* is an eloquent symbol for the state we enter when we begin to grow closer to God because he has begun to invade and possess our inner being.

John of the Cross made the term famous, but not necessarily understood. The dark night is much concerned with three special processes: bringing faith to the heroic level; waiting for God to take action; being cleansed of sin down to the deepest levels.

Because of the essential part faith plays, the dark night can also be called *the night of faith*.

The above processes cause all kinds of psychological and emotional, as well as spiritual disturbances within us. A sense of *dislocation* is a predominant one. There is a fracture in our inner being, and what takes place on one side of this fracture is foreign to what takes place on the other. While we go about the ordinary business of living, using our faculties as we are meant to use them and coping with everyday routine, another kind of living (or is it dying?) that we cannot define or locate, but know is there, is gradually evolving in some secret, inner strata of being.

Which is the real life? To which do we belong? Which duty belongs where? What are we meant to be attending to? What degree of intensity of our left hand not knowing what our right hand is doing can we bear without reaching the insanity of a genuine split personality?

Painfully, because it is a new process, we exercise faith to affirm our belief that this sense of dislocation is not a curse but a grace, that the transcendent God is truly immanent within us—somewhere, somehow, that this being so we must be safe, no matter how precarious we feel, that the best thing is to keep on doggedly praying, "Lord, I believe; please help my unbelief."

This experience of dislocation leads to greater humility if we face and accept our helplessness while we turn over our state trustingly to God.

Because reason cannot cope with and explain the invasion of God in the night of faith, a sense of absurdity also develops. The universe is not rational, but irrational. God disregards the laws of our beings, and chooses to deal capriciously with us, according to whim, making playthings of us.

This is what we feel.

Reason, which we once applied to the ordered street map of our lives to show us where to go next, is useless here. We have no sense of direction anymore and everything is an outlandish muddle. The bomb of God's presence has fallen among our planned streets to produce chaos. Apparently he has a reconstruction scheme, but he is certainly not revealing it yet.

We live in an inner world where paradoxes abound, ambiguities proliferate, contradictions erupt and day is night.

Some of the literature produced by the modern schools of black comedy and absurd drama graphically illustrate this state, though they may seem to be atheistic in content. Beckett's *Waiting for Godot* is particularly relevant. Because ours is an age of unfaith, it is prone to suffer psychological traumas similar to those induced by the night of faith. One wonders whether the dark night is not of much wider application in human life than has traditionally been taught. God, who usually moves in mysterious ways, is not confined within creed and dogma and may well utilize unbelief to bring about purgation and a philosophy of absurdity to teach the truth of humanity's relationship with the incomprehensible Absolute.

Many of the pronouncements of the death-of-God theologians could be regarded not so much as heresy as attempts to express the modern age's sense of absurdity and experience of the inscrutability and indefinability of God, an experience which mystics have often affirmed.

While reason is being crucified so are the emotions, for they often feel that God is alien and destructive, even an enemy, while faith continues to affirm he is friend, lover, creator and comforter. Experiencing one thing in the emotions while believing its opposite through faith intensifies the sense of dislocation and absurdity.

Another characteristic of this night is *impotence* in prayer—or just impotence.

Any pleasure or sweetness or even ease in prayer has given way to aridity which at times intensifies into active repugnance for and rebellion against prayer. The old ways of praying no longer work, and indeed have become impossible, and no new way has taken their place.

If an adviser says, "But you must pray!" the despairing reply is likely to be, "But I *can't* pray." The sufferer does not understand that what he or she should say is, "I can no longer pray in the ways I used to pray. They don't make sense any longer." What the adviser should say is, "Nevertheless, you must keep your appointment with God at the same regular times, even if you seem to be doing nothing as you wait on him."

We, the sufferers, long to pray, for we long to be with God, and in the past we have found that prayer often led to that sweet certainty of presence which is what we think we still need. We do not understand that such visitations occurred at a comparatively superficial level of being, and now God is calling us to an encounter in the hidden fastness of our inner temple of the Holy Spirit where the marriage union is to be finally consummated.

While we dumbly sense the call, we cannot define or answer it, nor can we find any way to bring about a meeting with the one who summons. Words seem totally inadequate, and at extreme times, idiotic. Feelings of devotion no longer rise up spontaneously to make prayer easy. Our state of numbness and dumbness makes us feel like mindless animals standing before a God who is hidden and refuses to communicate with us. At times we reach such a degree of impotence and insensibility that we seem to have become stones frozen in a glacier.

The frozen stone
it stands alone.
No bird will nest
no traveller rest
where comforts are
so few and far.

Such solitude
no man has made.
Another Will
ordained this still
denuded place
of chilly grace.

Said heart: I moan
to be a stone
where no bird nests
or traveller rests.
Said soul: The thaw
will come for sure.

At the same time as we cannot pray, we can find no distraction from the attempt to pray. We have already jettisoned so much on the *nada* path that there is nothing left that we can "get drunk" on. We may violently desire at times to find oblivion in something or someone, but we know too well how false and unsatisfying such oblivion would prove to be to one who aches for the oblivion of being lost in God.

Something of this sense of impotence, and also other aspects of the night of faith, are cleverly conveyed in Graham Greene's presentation of Querry in *A Burntout Case*. Is this man an atheist or so deeply involved with God that he has passed beyond knowing into unknowing? Is his impotence that of a love too intense to express itself, or of an indifference too profound to cause any ripple of emotion or involvement?

Whatever it is that Greene means to convey in his characteristically ambiguous manner, those in the night of faith will find the comfort of the familiar in his description of Querry's interior state.

Impotence in prayer is caused by the fact that the night of faith is the beginning of contemplation. We can find no way out of this choking fog that has come down upon the *nada* path to immobilize us, hiding every familiar landmark. The thick darkness can seem so impenetrable as to be claustrophobic.

It is as if we are incarcerated in a pitch dark dungeon round the unyielding walls of which we continually feel for signs of a door, a window, or even a crack, but without ever finding one. Our very fingertips become insensible in the process.

It is no use shouting, for the fog and walls muffle the voice so that it has no more resonance and carrying power than a whisper. And, anyway, who or what is there to hear if we do shout? No one and nothing.

The impenetrable darkness hides a void. It is a void as vast as the infinity of space. Even to think of it terrifies the mind and heart. To launch out into it would be spiritual suicide. And anyway, it is impossible because of the dungeon.

In such a situation, lost and nightbound, impotent and dumb, threatened by absurdity and the void, unable to escape from the dungeon, what is the pilgrim on the *nada* path to do? Often all he or she can do is wait and endure.

Here is an analogy for what this idiotic waiting is like: The place is a small, wayside station in the middle of nowhere. The tracks are rusty and weeds grow between the ties. The wind sighs gently in the long grasses and in the trees that border the depot. The station master went on vacation aeons ago.

There seem to be no other passengers. No one passes along the dusty, country road or calls out from the warehouse nearby. A bus stands idle and empty near the platform. Tattered posters flap in the wind and the timetable hanging in the small waiting room with its wooden seat fixed round the walls has no visible relation to reality.

Soul is stranded here and can't quite recall how or when. There is only a formless kind of memory of a time when life was different, there being obvious meaning and purpose, definite direction, and a comfortable sense of aiming at and attaining goals. Then Soul was in the mainstream and on the move, alive, in touch with things, busy, effective and motivated.

Ah, yes . . .

But at some stage Soul is rather vague about (could he have been mildly intoxicated—drugged—half asleep perhaps?), his purposeful, planned journey was interrupted (he can't quite remember—was it foggy?—or the middle of the night?) and he got off (or was put off) at this station. As far as he remembers (but there is a distressing vagueness about his mental processes these days), he thought when he got off the train that he had reached some important junction. He was going to change trains and set off again on his methodical itinerary.

At first (so wrapped up in his own self-importance was he), he scarcely noticed the silence and emptiness of the place, the absence of fellow travellers, the desolate unkemptness, the air of being in the middle of nowhere in the center of nothingness. But gradually, as the days, weeks, months and years passed, he had to face reality and see it for what it was.

There were so few distractions that he had plenty of time to think. Could it be called thinking? Realizing, anyway. He had plenty of time to realize what he was and what his position was, and finally he arrived at certain conclusions . . .

He is a nobody, of no account whatever. He must be. If he weren't, someone would remember him and rescue him. A busy train would come puffing along, an important official would alight and come up to him, bright with good cheer and apologies.

"Why, old man, we had no idea you were stranded here. As soon as the rumor reached us we got moving straight away. We couldn't leave someone like *you* moldering away in a place like *this*. Come on, let's get on our way. We've all kinds of plans and you play an absolutely indispensable part. The sooner we get going, the better."

A pleasant fantasy—but the fact is that no train comes and no official appears to tell him he is indispensable. On the contrary, he is obviously highly dispensable. No one even remembers his existence. The busy world functions somewhere or other quite effectively in spite of his absence. The plans are made without his advice. The campaigns are conducted minus his renowned audacity, resourcefulness and intelligence.

And regarding these latter—he doesn't seem to possess them any longer. He can't think of a single plan to escape from his present predicament. He is eaten up with hesitancy and lack of confidence.

One day he decides to set off hitchhiking—anything, anything to be on the move. But he gets no further than the gate into the railway yards. For one thing, what use to hitchhike on a road that never has any traffic?

Another time he decides to escape across country, but he no sooner reaches the fence than he realizes he'll get hopelessly lost without a map—and anyway a train just might be coming up the line way back there. Better not leave, just in case.

Another time, so intense is his boredom that he takes out his razor and decides to slit his throat, remembering just in time that instead of solving anything that will set him off on another journey far, far more terrible than this. He is frightened that his reason could be so clouded even for a moment—but it's this endless waiting, this uncertainty, this deadness.

He decides to form a plan for retracing his route. He'll go back to where he came from and begin all over again, but just as he picks up his bag to set off he realizes that he hasn't the least idea whether he came from up or down the line.

The general deduction from all this is that as well as being a nobody, he knows nothing. It's true he can read the timetable (though his concentration is so poor these days that he has to keep on going back over it to find out just what it was he read a moment ago), but he has no idea how to apply it to himself. It seems to bear no relation to him. Either it is idiotic, or he is. And anyway, nothing it predicts ever happens. Not to him, that is. Maybe it happens to other people in other places, but not to him in this place.

Whatever this place is. Wherever it is. *If* it is . . .

Sometimes he wonders if he's asleep and it's all a dream, sometimes if he's mad and it's all an illusion, sometimes if he's neurotic and the victim of an obsession—and there's no doubt he's under the influence of a compulsion.

What is this compulsion?

It's the compulsion to wait.

Soul is waiting. He has to wait.

What or who is he waiting for?

He knows really, but it's a kind of knowledge that's in his blood and heart rather than in his head. He can't think logically about it, or make theories, or base a plan of action on it. But if someone were to appear (Someone appear? Impossible! Such joy and easement is beyond imagining!) and say to him, "You've been here a long time. What are you doing?" he'd answer, without thinking, "I'm waiting."

The other would say, "What are you waiting for?"

"I'm waiting for someone."

"Who?"

"I'm waiting for God."

Yes, of course . . . that's what it is! He forgets in the confusing maze of sameness that dulls him into an imbecilic calm. But that is what he's doing. That must be the purpose of his being here.

This meaningless existence has a meaning, and it is to wait. It has a purpose, and it is to wait for God. This vacancy and lack of direction, this intense loneliness and monotony, this abandonment by the whole world (and by God) is something after all. It is "waiting for God." That's its name. That's what it *is*.

This realization brings him a certain bare comfort. Making a little joke with himself about everything having its use if only you can discover it, he goes and sits down in the waiting room instead of pacing the platform and gazing up and down the line. There's a room for waiting, so he might as well use it for waiting.

"What am I doing? Waiting . . . Who am I waiting for? God." He repeats the lesson over and over like a child. In fact, in many ways he feels he has returned to the helplessness and dependence of childhood. Children are left to wait in all kinds of places by their parents, and since they have neither the strength nor knowledge nor resourcefulness to shift, they just have to wait till they're rescued. It's no use having opinions or desires of their own. They have to depend on others.

"I don't have to do anything," Soul reassures himself. Indeed, he can't do anything. "I just have to wait. That's my work. Waiting. Waiting is my work. My work is waiting. Lord, help me to wait well. Help me to wait patiently and in peace."

Sitting there composedly, he begins to develop a philosophy of waiting, making necessity the mother of invention. But he finds that, though these thoughts are interesting and help to while away the time, the most helpful thing of all is to turn his waiting into prayer. It takes him quite a while to work out a way of doing this, but once he has it, he finds it brings him peace. The peace is dry and empty, but it is undoubtedly peace.

"In his will is my peace," Soul learns to say. He means it, though he finds he hasn't much at all to say to God. His prayer of waiting isn't a wordy one. There's no eloquence about it. Often it consists only of saying over and over, "God—God—God . . ." He finds rest simply in resting in God. He develops a technique of abandoning his whole being and all his life (life? here?) to God.

He begins to understand that the circumstances of his life are God's will for him. God has put him here. God keeps him here. God is going to move him from here when it is his will. It is God's will, God's time, God's purpose, that matter.

Soul realizes that he, being a nobody who knows nothing, can't expect to fathom God's ways, but what he *can* do is trust them.

Through practice, he develops a facility in abandoning himself in trust to this state that is God's will for him, even of willing it because God wills it. Strange, but this brings him a queer, passionless joy. He is happy without feeling happiness. He is at peace without experiencing peacefulness.

He has found the purpose for his life as he must live it here and now. The purpose is waiting for God.

The Wanderer

I have nothing enlightening to say about this journey
save parched bones in the sand, torrid winds,
and the monotony of thoughts like camel-trains,
heavy, lethargic plodders, trudging
one after one, patiently resentful
of the bales of my inert desires.

Other travellers could no doubt tell you
about the exhilaration of making port
in unfamiliar harbors, the tumult,
the traffic and the clamor, barter of commodities
and all the busy interchange of trade.
I only know the terrain of the desert.

Where I make my way the feet
of pilgrims have trodden out a thread of path
almost indiscernible among the stones and sand.
Nothing grows. Sparse, stunted shrubs
are fossilized by the dry wind's hostility.
This is not the place where the manna fell.

Other travellers might well mention
the fascinating turbulence of foreign cities,
monuments of creamy stone pale in the dawn,
great rivers like primordial snakes,
corn waving to their brinks, and slow barges heavy with grain.
I cannot boast of even one oasis.

The way I came by is obliterated.
The way ahead is lost among the stones.
The mirage of a face that smiles, of hands
that touch in love, cannot distract
my automatic feet from motion.
These stones also will not be turned to bread.

4 Irrelevancies and Puerilities

JOHN OF THE CROSS is always systematic; if at times convoluted and abstract he is also practical and blunt.

He conceives of the dark night as the gradual penetration of the Spirit through the upper layers of the soul down to its innermost, hidden depths. We can facilitate this process by deliberately practicing virtue and curbing our actions and inclinations that are anything but virtuous—hence his term "the active night."

However, the deepest and most thorough penetrations have to be done by the Spirit at work in us while we remain in a state of receptive passivity. These penetrations he calls "the passive purgations." As they operate in us, they pass first through the upper layers of the senses. Then they plunge below these into the more significant areas where the same kinds of human missing-the-mark occur, but spiritually.

The *Dark Night of the Soul* opens with a masterly examination of "the faults of beginners" (beginners in contemplation), which St. John bundles together as "irrelevancies and puerilities." However, when we ponder them and examine our own inner selves and outer conduct in the light of them, it becomes glaringly evident that most of them operate in one way or another in our own lives.

This is chastening! As he means it to be.

He takes care to warn us that "however assiduously the beginner practices the mortification in himself (in the active night) of all these actions and passions of his, he can never completely succeed—very far from it—until God shall work it in him passively by means of the purgation of the said night" (*D.N.* I,VII,5).

In Book I of *Dark Night*, which treats of the night of sense, St. John has his own systematic exposition of the penetration and making spiritually healthy of the soul's upper layers. This concerns mortifying and pacifying the contents of the "house of sense."

35

Those led into the dark night are already contemplatives, pilgrims on the apophatic way and *nada* path, but they have many imperfections, weaknesses and bad habits. These must be dealt with before full union with the Trinity can come about.

The virtues acquired in the active nights have to be tested and strengthened. Though in one sense "beginners" are advanced in the spiritual life and solidly established in virtue, they are in another immature and feeble when compared with those who have submitted to the deeper, passive purifications and attained transforming union.

Though they have suffered, striven and gained much, they still have a long way to travel on the *nada* path and much to suffer before they reach the summit of this Mountain of Love.

John analyzes their state in terms of the seven capital sins: pride, avarice, luxury, wrath, gluttony, envy, sloth—all considered in relation to spirituality, not as gross sins of the flesh. These have long been eliminated.

Pride

As beginners in contemplation we have within us a secret self-satisfaction and vanity that makes us think we can teach and criticize others, even our confessors and directors. Our pharisaism causes spiritual pride in our gifts and virtues, while at the same time we are anxious for praise and esteem. Touchy over correction or criticism, we easily nurse resentment against our critics while we burn with desire to justify ourselves.

We engage in little dramas to impress others, preferring our ecstasies and fervors to take place in public so others will notice and be impressed.

We insinuate ourselves with our confessors, hoping to be their favorites and falsifying our confessions to give a better impression. We excuse rather than accuse ourselves, magnifying our virtues and minimizing our imperfections.

Disheartenment and even dismay occurs when we do catch a glimpse of what we are really like, for we had imagined ourselves holier by far than this. Our motives for wanting to be cleansed of faults have more to do with self-love than pure longing to glorify God by a holy life. Self-love also drives us to a restless ambition to be always visibly climbing higher to get to the top quickly. For God's sake or our own? This is the crucial question.

We compare ourselves with others, to our own secret advantage. Comparisons in the spiritual life are always unwise and too often uncharitable also, because only God knows anyone's secret heart. They are particularly odious when we make them ourselves in our own favor and another's disfavor. Sincere, protracted efforts to combat spiritual pride usually result in our being able to control obvious expressions of self-adulation and mortify blatant efforts to put ourselves on display as a shining example of virtue for all to emulate.

But the roots of fascination with our own unique splendor and consequent denigration of others remain undisturbed. It is of little importance whether psychological mechanisms of over-compensation and inferiority-superiority syndromes are involved or not. God has pity on the evil effects on us of a flawed nature and nurture, but this cannot alter the fact that spiritual pride in any form is an insult to truth.

"What have you that you have not received?"

We may glibly answer from a surface sincerity, "Nothing"— yet we are not purified until we gain that true assessment of our bankruptcy that comes only from our witnessing the Spirit's pitilessly probing searchlight playing upon the latest statement of our position sent us by the divine banker.

The covert conviction that we are humbly self-effacing saints as yet unrecognized by the spiritually insensitive mob has to be uncovered and faced for what it is.

The more secret a form of self-love, the more dangerous it is, and the more drastic the means necessary for its radical removal. Only the celestial surgeon is competent to undertake such operations, and he does so in the passive purgations.

Those with pure intentions advance much more quickly because in their humility they have "very little satisfaction with themselves; they consider all others as far better, and usually have a holy envy of them, and an eagerness to serve God as they do" (*D.N.* I,II,6).

Never satisfied with their own efforts, these humble ones minimize them and are occupied so earnestly with doing better that they have no time to criticize others. In fact, they are pleased when they themselves are despised and depreciated, because their humility sees this as the result of others' just assessment of them. "It seems to

them strange that anyone should say these good things of them"
(*D.N.* I,II,6).

Eager to learn from others, they have no need to be or to prove
themselves right, so they refrain from clever comments and astute
rationalizations. They are even anxious to have their faults and sins
pointed out to them, because they are so sincere and humble in their
desire to do better and please God.

"These souls will give their heart's blood to anyone that serves
God, and will help others to serve him as much as in them lies. The
imperfections into which they see themselves fall they bear with humility, meekness of spirit and a loving fear of God, hoping in him"
(*D.N.* I,II,8).

The result is that they are led more quickly to a closer degree of
union because they are so receptive and lack the arrogance and high
self-opinion of those on whom spiritual pride has a strong hold.

Avarice

The spiritually avaricious are "discontented with the spirituality which God gives them" (*D.N.* I,III,1). They want something
different, just like people who always want to keep up with the
Joneses, acquiring material goods not because they genuinely need
them, but in order to impress others and enhance their own sense of
self-worth.

These grumblers are always looking for new forms of spirituality. Though they read spiritual books greedily, they never seriously
apply in a personal way what they find there. Varied and even bizarre religious objects adorn their persons and their homes, and
they are always wanting to acquire more of these. Their attachment is to the accidents rather than to the substance of devotion.
Their understanding is confused and fragmented, lacking the poverty of spirit, simplicity and austerity that has no need to surround
itself with all this paraphernalia, because it is aware it bears the
Trinity within itself.

The really spiritual are indifferent to such possessions, longing
to please God by relying on him, and not to please themselves by
indulging in such childishness.

The spiritually avaricious also succumb to querulousness and
depression because they no longer experience consolation and pleasure in the practice of virtue and in prayer. They lack poverty of

spirit, which considers only the substance of devotion, for they let themselves be preoccupied with a wistful, restless desire for the flowery, imposing accidents.

They may even indulge in counterfeiting what God withholds from them, whipping up a feeling of devotion with accompanying sighs, tears, anguished looks and seraphic smiles. When this does not give the emotional fulfillment they seek, they become down-hearted. It does not seem possible that this dry, unsatisfying, monotonous, boring non-prayer could be God's will for them, his chosen.

Perhaps they are guilty of some monstrous infidelity? Perhaps he has abandoned them? Perhaps they have taken a wrong turning and must go back?

Perhaps their whole idea of the spiritual life is deluded? If only God would relent and let them experience even a minor ecstasy or an infinitesimal levitation or a not-too-obtrusive access of holy ardor, or a transport or two, or a locution.

After such reassurance, they tell him, they would complain no more, having sweet memories with which to fill the barren hours.

It does not occur to them that the too familiarly trite saying about loving the consolations of God instead of the God of consolations could possibly apply to them.

Luxury

Those at this stage of the spiritual life no longer commit deliberate sins of bodily sensuality, but they do have involuntary "impure acts and motions in the sensual part of the soul" (*D.N.* I,IV,1).

There is a kind of softness and voluptuousness about feelings and experiences tainted by luxury, by attachment to what is desirable, but not indispensable. These indicate enjoyment in pleasure for its own sake, coupled with an emotional lushness signifying treacherous, marshy terrain hidden beneath an inviting surface.

Luxury encourages delusion, rationalization, romanticism and self-cosseting. It weakens the will, fosters emotionality (as distinct from hearty, healthy emotion) and lowers spiritual tone. It is compatible with outward austerity and materially poor surroundings, which at this stage of the spiritual life have often been willingly embraced, for it is more often an indulgence of the feelings than of the flesh.

Uprisings of sensual thoughts, images, impulses, rebellions, may come about even during prayer or at Mass. The devil's involvement may provoke severe distress, for he presents sensual fantasies "that are most foul and impure, and at times very closely related to certain spiritual things and persons that are of profit to their souls" (D.N. I,IV,3).

The result is a temptation to discouragement, to give up prayer for fear of being assaulted in this way again. There is often depression and lack of will to oppose the Devil of Negativity, combined with an obsessive dread of giving in and so sinning.

Sometimes intense consolations can arouse similar sensual thoughts and even physical reactions that cause pleasure that is anything but purely spiritual. In fact, almost any strong emotional upheaval such as anger or grief could cause a reaction in over-imaginative, hypersensitive and perhaps rather weakminded people.

Another danger in this area is making "friendships of a spiritual kind with others, which oftentimes arise from luxury and not from spirituality" (D.N. I,IV,7).

We feel that, deprived of so much in so many other ways, and especially of pleasure in God, we can at least permit ourselves a personal relationship that involves mutual fascination and sensuous pleasure in another's physical presence, touch or gaze. There is no sin involved, we reassure ourselves.

And yet we cannot get rid of this sense of being half smothered in a feather eiderdown smelling strongly of vanilla essence.

This is an ambivalent area, but John gives a sure sign of the holiness of a relationship, which is similar to the one Teresa gives, though she affirms "spiritual-sensible" relationships are good, in spite of the emotional element, as long they help one grow closer to God.

John says, "When the friendship is purely spiritual, the love of God grows with it; and the more the soul remembers it, the more it remembers the love of God, and the greater the desire it has for God; so that, as one grows, the other grows also" (D.N. I,IV,7).

These are wise words. To live by them requires self-control, delicacy of conscience, bleak honesty with oneself and the other. and submission to God's will in all things.

When sensuality is the source of love between friends, it causes a disturbance in the spiritual life characterized by forgetfulness and even indifference toward God as the friends become more and more obsessively preoccupied with each other. There is uneasiness of conscience and a general tendency toward lukewarmness in religious practice and the virtues.

Wrath

Wrath is the opposite of spiritual temperance and sobriety. It causes bitterness, resentment, restlessness, disappointment and annoyance when consolations in prayer do not, or cease to occur, and one does not become a saint instantaneously.

Those influenced by wrath also become irritated at others' sins and are fond of keeping an eye on them. The same attitudes may be shown toward their own shortcomings and failure to make progress, though who but God can ever measure "progress"?

In spite of devising all kinds of demanding resolutions about what they will do to satisfy their over-eagerness to arrive among the front few, the spiritually wrathful are hindered by their own lack of patience and meekness. They cannot wait for God to bring about in his own way and time what in his knowledge is best for them as a help to holiness. They have yet to learn to be passive under God's action and to wait for his will to evince itself.

An urgent desire to reach the heights of unitive love in one exhilarating bound of impressive self-denial and magnanimous cleaving to the cross can result in an acid disillusionment when they undeniably prove to be the tortoise, not the hare.

Someone must be to blame. It can't be ourselves, for our generosity and enthusiasm are undeniable. Is it God then? Has he implanted false expectations in us, only to gloat over their frustration? Is it this, that or the other person who has failed us in some way? Not given inspiration, encouragement, example? Who has been bestowing criticism on us where it is not due?

It does not occur to us that God, being infinite wisdom, knows best and at what time and rate we should advance, and also whether we shall benefit spiritually more from consolation or from aridity. In effect, we have an imperative desire to be at the wheel ourselves, deciding both upon the route and speed.

All this reveals that we have yet a great deal to learn about being passive while God acts in and on us. We are not yet capable of believing that he can drive the car better than we can and knows all the routes and maps by heart.

Gluttony

Sweetness and consolation in the earlier stages of the spiritual life may continue to be hungered and even craved for after God has removed them and is demanding a more mature way of serving him. Those hankering after what they no longer receive may become peevish and lukewarm. If anyone tries to restrain or redirect them, they insist they themselves know what is best for them and an unkind God has deprived them of it.

Those indulging in spiritual gluttony may express it, strangely enough, by an addiction to penances of an extreme kind, prolonged fasts and other activities that suggest at least an element of sado-masochism. They hope to provoke spiritual experiences by bodily macerations taken to the extreme, for it is known ecstasies can be caused by such.

If any sweetness or pleasure does alleviate their aridity, they seize on it gluttonously, anxious to savor every drop to the full, reluctant to relinquish it, careful to relive and re-experience it over and over in the memory afterward, while they long for it to come again even more intensely.

Thus they reveal their lack of spiritual temperance and sobriety. They would be the peacock, not the dove. They would be drunk, not sober.

Their behavior indicates self-will and pride at work, together with a lack of discretion, resignation, obedience, abandonment, right reason and good sense. When what they hope for does not occur and they are left in darkness and aridity, they complain against God and consider giving up. They "think that their own satisfaction and pleasure are the satisfaction and service of God" (D.N. I,IV,3).

They are always trying to wring some kind of sensible pleasure out of all their religious exercises, even attendance at Mass and reception of Communion. If no pleasure results they rebel; they cannot rest in God's will in blind faith, accepting what he sends or does not send them as the best possible thing for them at this time.

Spiritual self-denial is not part of their program. They are like children continually whining and begging for sweets. Because they have little self-control, they blindly follow their inclinations rather than seeking God's will in all things.

Spiritual Envy and Sloth

These cause us to feel displeasure at the spiritual advancement and experiences of others, because, by comparison, we see ourselves deprived of them and left behind. We suffer disheartenment and even grief that others have sped past us on the *nada* path, and envy and regret when we hear them praised. They are occupying the place meant for us; they are getting the recognition and applause that rightly belong to us, and we feel bitter and mean about it.

In contrast, we should be feeling "holy envy, comprising grief at not having the virtues of others, yet also joy because others have them, and delight when others outstrip us in the service of God, wherein we ourselves are so remiss" (*D.N.* I,VII,1).

We give in to the meannness of disparaging and criticizing those who are being praised while we are overlooked, though we are careful and clever enough to do it in some subtle way that will not make obvious either to ourselves or them the secret spite we feel, our anxious desire to pull down to our level those who surpass us.

We even feel such spite against God. He does not give us any sweetness and consolation in prayer, so we will pay him out by giving up prayer. Sloth, joining with envy, causes us to abandon our efforts to please God in prayer and action, or else we continue unwillingly and halfheartedly. We do not appreciate and will not submit to the way of negation of our will and pleasure for God's sake. We want "God to will that which we ourselves will, and are fretful at having to will that which he wills, and find it repugnant to accommodate our will to that of God" (*D.N.* I,VII,3).

We are very far from being humble servants, let alone slaves of God as our Lord and Master was, yet we are largely oblivious of our intransigence, rationalizing about it, so that we would be genuinely shocked if told we had little love and less docility.

We are like small children who say pettishly, "If you don't do as I say, I'm not going to play anymore," and then retire to a corner to sulk.

It can be seen how all the above are in some way linked with pride, self-love and self-will.

Even while we are observing and congratulating ourselves on our progress along the *nada* path, these deep-seated hindrances, like invisible, very strong nylon ropes attached to poles sunk in the ground, are holding us back in ways we do not even see until the dark contemplation of the passive purgations reveals them to us.

"There still remain in the spirit the stains of the old man, although the spirit thinks not that this is so, neither can it perceive them" (*D.N.* II,II,1).

Even though we are strongly grounded in virtue, and genuinely anxious to please God, this "old man" still causes us to pride ourselves, more or less surreptitiously, on our spiritual gifts and even to make a show of them before others, hoping to impress them and be taken for a saint, or at least for someone who is unusually interesting spiritually and worth cultivating.

Such lack of humility encourages delusions. Because we want to believe we are chosen and unique, we readily interpret as special gifts from God and signs of his favor what are really the products of our own imagination and desire, or even of the devil. In colloquial terms we still have big ideas about ourselves, and think God should do as we command in order to bring them to fruition. We stop being careful to decrease so that Christ may increase in us, and begin to build up a spiritual bank balance for ourselves, gloating over our assets and attributing them to our own efforts.

And so various forms of presumption and pride, and various ways of clinging to God's gifts instead of only and always to God himself, still hamper us, preventing our further progress until we are disencumbered of them, becoming both much simpler and more honest. Humility is truth. The passive purgations teach humility through truth, and truth through humility.

The *nada* path is safely traversed only in dark and pure faith. The nights of the passive purgations are coterminous with the night of faith in which God himself is sought, rather than any of his gifts or manifestations, no matter how sublime and beautiful.

We must acknowledge that however beautiful and reverent the forms of worship that we made in our inner temple to God, no matter how we thought we understood and experienced God, it was mostly a kind of childishness. And the time comes when childish things must be put away. We have not been on Tabor, but in a state of auto-intoxication on some slight elevation bounded by our own backyard. God himself is above and beyond all this. It must be transcended if we are to go on to the heights. Only then will God cleanse us from "all these irrelevancies and puerilities" so that we at last grow to full maturity in Christ.

"In poverty, and without protection or support in all the apprehensions of my soul—that is, in the darkness of my understanding and the constraint of my will, in affliction and anguish with respect to memory, remaining in the dark in pure faith, which is dark night for the said natural faculties, the will alone being touched by grief and afflictions and yearnings for the love of God—I went forth from myself—that is, from my low manner of understanding, from my weak mode of loving and from my poor and limited manner of experiencing God, without being hindered therein by sensuality or the devil" (*D.N.* II,IV,1).

Death and Rebirth

It takes a long time to die.
You are dying even while
you are learning how to come alive and be.

On its bed of nails, inert,
lies what will be the corpse,
or else it wanders mesmerized in circles
tremulously fingering familiar objects,
dazed, entangled in confusion,
clawed at by ancient, rooted agonies
persistently invading spaces
up till now inviolate from their raids.

Seeking relief, it stumbles back to bed,
curls in the fetal posture, instinctively assured
such small exposure of its surfaces
will mean less piercing of their vulnerabilities.
It lies there cradling its omnivorous pain
arms crossed protectively on breast
knees hunched to meet them—
a tightly rolled up ball of dread
hoping to be invincible when most at risk.

> At last, enfeebled into acquiescence,
> it yields to the invaders, accepts defeat, and,
> face to wall, it dies . . .

> Your old self lies there like the husk
> from which the butterfly has just emerged.

You seem to rest and sleep. You dream . . .

Teresa's transformed silkworm spreads
its iridescent wings set free to soar
in palpitating life. It settles
on a gleaming flower and sucks its honey.
Cocoons are now forgotten. This liberation
intoxicates, infusing such huge torrents
of new life it almost shudders it apart.
The safe confinement of the husk is gone for ever.
Tremendous gales may come to tear its wings
yet in its carefree joy it takes no heed
of that or any other threat.

> You have become this butterfly.
> You live and soar and have your being
> in him who is your home. And never
> will you die that death again, for though
> it was the end, through it you were reborn.

5 Manna in the Wilderness

W<small>E HAVE EXAMINED</small> the faults of those who are just entering the state of contemplation and the passive purgations of the sense. This state, John tells us, "is common and comes to many—these are the beginners," whereas the passive night of the spirit "is the portion of very few" (*D.N.* I, VIII, 1).

This second night is a deepening and intensification of the first, so that examination of the first is important if we wish to understand and recognize the second. However, I shall deal only briefly with the first, as it is the second which brings the soul to sanctity. Our inner being is one continuous realm which is not compartmentalized, though it helps to consider it as such at times.

Until we enter the night of sense, we have not fully realized that love of God and neighbor is a matter of deliberate choice. Whether it involves emotion (the "sensible") or not is irrelevant, just as it is irrelevant whether or not there is felt consolation in prayer.

We choose to love God as he has chosen to love us. As soon as we open our heart to his love, he begins to give it to us to love others with. At baptism we were incorporated into divine love, but as we mature we have to choose to accept and live out the consequences of that incorporation.

Involved in the extended incarnation and continuous passion as we are, also through baptism, we yet have to become conscious of the implications and possibilities of this living union with Christ. In that developing awareness we deliberately take the step of faith that means we acknowledge our personal, willed responsibility to live in and for that union. As we continue in the way of willed love, we shall keep on discovering deeper and deeper levels of possible commitment. Whether we advance, withdraw, or try simply to stay where we are (which is impossible) will determine our degree of love-union with the Trinity.

When in the course of the sincere, continual practice of loving and doing God's will to our utmost, certain signs become apparent, we know that we have entered the passive night of sense. These signs are as follows:

We are not getting from our relationship with God, our efforts to please him, and our prayer, any pleasure, consolation or sense of achievement, and this aridity has been constant for a considerable time, that is, it is not the result of some passing emotional crisis, ill-health or fatigue.

While we remain unsatisfied by God, we realize that, at the same time, nothing and no one else satisfies us either. We may try to find fulfillment in pleasure, work, personal relationships, and the rest, but any experience of completion is temporary and minor. Only God can meet our need—we know that—and yet God seems unattainable.

Our state is not the result of unfaithfulness or acedia, because we persist in the effort to do God's will in all matters. At the same time we often suffer painful doubts about whether we are falling short of what he wants of us, and whether our aridity and emptiness are not caused by our own lack of perseverance. We continually watch ourselves for signs of backsliding and carefully renew our resolutions.

St. John assures us that this distressing state results from the fact that God has begun to feed the soul secretly with contemplation. It is as yet too delicate and tentative to flood our awareness, or induce any emotion or even consciousness of its presence, yet at the same time we find it impossible to meditate as before, to reflect on the truths of the faith during prayer, or purposefully to relate our emotions to the things of God so that we experience sweetness, delight and the assurance of having accomplished something measurable.

We are like the Israelites in the wilderness who are being fed by God with manna, but cannot accustom their palates to it. The taste is too indefinable, strange and almost non-existent. They long for the food they are used to, with all its strong flavors and recognizable stimulants.

Yet the manna is real and it does sustain life.

God, at work in our mysterious depths, is producing effects on the memory, understanding and will that we cannot control and must accept passively. He is weaning us from the familiar and introducing us to something quite alien and incomprehensible.

Though both intellect and emotions have become numb and incapable of functioning in relation to God, the longing to pray and
be near him remains. Compelled to seek solitude and silence, the
soul is yet tortured by the sense of God's absence rather than presence.

We are on a real starvation diet, which, providing there is no
deliberate sin in our lives and we are not in a state of depression or
bodily illness, is really a special grace to thank God for. We do not
feel like thanking him for it, but we choose to do so because we trust
his action. All the same, there is great need of an understanding director who can provide reassurance at this time.

The inability to meditate and reflect arouses a dread that we
have collapsed weakly into lukewarmness. We fear that God is punishing us for some dreadful sin of which we are not even aware.
Anxiety that our wills have become severed from his and we have
been "cast into outer darkness" causes us grief. Our need is to calm
all this unrest and fear and stay very still and quiet in God's presence, hidden in darkness and aridity, accepting them without question or disturbance. A wise, knowledgeable director can be of great
help to us at this stage.

God is drawing closer, and as a result we are enveloped in
apophatic emptiness and obscurity. "Humankind cannot bear very
much reality" (T.S. Eliot)—and it is Reality itself that is invading
us. To let ourselves be troubled by the strangeness and become desolate at the loss of sweetness is to impede the divine penetration. If
we struggle to return to meditation, we shall also slow down the
development of contemplation. It is now God's turn to labor, and
ours to let him act.

This "letting act" and "letting be" is a good deal harder to do
than might seem apparent. The surgeon analogy helps. He is at
work (anesthetics being unavailable) on our deepest wounds. Only
our heroic trust in his expertise, plus our own determination, will
enable us to stay still. Luckily God, in his compassionate love, pours
invisible torrents of grace into the wounds he both tends and makes.
Thus he helps us to endure in the darkness of faith.

"Contemplation is naught else than a secret, peaceful and loving infusion from God, which, if it be permitted, enkindles the soul
with the spirit of love" (*D.N.* I,X,6).

The trouble is those imperfections, our own particular, invol-

untary versions of the seven deadly sins, persist in getting in the way
and hindering us from giving our full permission. We are, in fact,
being prepared to enter the night of spirit, if we prove strong and
willing enough to endure it. Our aridity is the sign of our immense,
consuming thirst for God that increases as we are divested of our
attachments to the not-God.

This is the night of purgation of desire. After it has done its
work, in both sense and spirit, all we shall be capable of desiring is
God and his will.

God is teaching us humility as we painfully learn the truth that
without him we can do nothing. Deprivation leaves us "empty and
disencumbered" (*D.N.* I,XII,4), so that all the time more and more
room is made for the Trinity to make its home in us. The "irrelevancies and puerilities" (and later, their very roots) are being cast out
like so much rubbish in a vigorous spring cleaning. There is a void
opening up within us, and it is being filled with Christ's living waters, which in turn will flow forth from us for others, to do his redemptive work of love. They will also ease our own aridity.

In our poverty and need we now find little cause to criticize and
judge our neighbor. We heartily endorse the publican's prayer, and
are too busy practicing it to be poking about to find the splinter in
anyone else's eye. We no longer experience ourselves as favorites, or
chosen, or the elect, or spiritually privileged, or capable of counsel-
ling others.

We become submissive, obedient, meek, content with our starvation diet, all gluttony purged from us. We do not seek our own
will, for we fear that it will lead us astray in the weakness of which
we are now so painfully and constantly aware. We covet nothing,
let alone our former pleasures in prayer, for the contemplative insight has made us suspicious of all that we once craved for and that
delighted us.

"God alone. . . . God alone . . . Give me God alone," is now
the constant entreaty of our hearts. In contrast to him, all else seems
tawdry and ephemeral.

Because God's action quells the urges of concupiscence, spiritual
tranquillity and peace gradually replace the restlessness, dissatisfac-
tion, instability of purpose and uprisings of the passions of joy, hope,
fear and grief that it at first caused in us. Instead we grow in charity
and purity of intention as we develop a positive taste for the delicate

manna with which the Spirit is feeding our spirits. This food arouses nothing in our emotions, and yet we are sure a grace has been received at a far deeper and more productive level than ever before.

Our soul rejoices at its release from bondage into "liberty of spirit, whereby in ever greater degree it gains the twelve fruits of the Holy Spirit" (*D.N.* I,XIII,11). As a reminder, and to show how they counter the "irrelevancies and puerilities," I list them: love, joy, peace, patient endurance, kindness, generosity, faith, fidelity, mildness, tolerance, chastity, self-control (see Gal 5:22-23).

When all this reorganizing and casting out has been accomplished, the house of sensuality is at last at rest and mortified. Those who reach this "rest" enter the way of progressives, proficients, illumination (which, paradoxically, means the dark-light that faith gives), infused contemplation. This is a stable state where spiritual peace is seldom deeply disturbed, and virtues are no longer difficult to practice, where awareness of being in the presence of God is constant, and abandonment and love well developed.

However, though these proficients may seem to have reached full and perfect love-union, they have not. For that, the passive night of spirit is necessary. In this the very roots of all the tendencies toward sin are attacked by grace and eliminated. Here God works at the deepest levels, in the unconscious, and the consequent agonies, upheavals, turbulences and temptations are so violent that the most heroic fortitude and abandonment are needed to endure and survive them sane.

"The night which we have called that of sense may and should be called a kind of correction and restraint of the desire rather than purgation. The reason is that all the imperfections and disorders of the sensual part have their strength and root in the spirit, where all habits, both good and bad, are brought into subjection, and thus, until these are purged, the rebellions and depravities of sense cannot be purged thoroughly" (*D.N.* II,III, 1).

In modern psychological parlance we might think of this as the process whereby grace pierces the conscious level of our inner being so as to plunge into the unconscious at its deepest strata. Here exist, unknown to us, all those repressions, complexes, psychological syndromes and submerged tendencies that influence our behavior, promote emotional upheavals and aberrations, and often reduce us to impotence before their insidious infiltrations or violent upsurges.

Grace operating in these profound, mysterious strata in the night of spirit gradually reveals to us what we need to know about ourselves in order to advance in love, brings under its control those so potent forces of primal energy, and casts out whatever can never be reconciled to God. It is no wonder that those in the deeper passive purgations often feel they are being psychologically and spiritually dismembered.

The process is certainly like profound, prolonged depth analysis, no matter what school of psychological thought it is conducted under.

John teaches that few go through this second night in this life. Those that God destines for it suffer much more deeply and more comprehensively in the night of sense. In their case the purifications of sense are so severe that it is almost impossible to distinguish them from those of the night of the spirit. For these souls the two nights are apt to be coterminous. They interlock and are superimposed like a multi-dimensional picture.

The higher God means to raise these chosen ones, the more utterly he humbles and humiliates them, and the more drastically he purges them of the weaknesses and sinful tendencies of sense.

The Land I Know

This is the land I know—the wasteland,
the inhospitable, frost-bitten zone
where the sun smites like a punishing fist
and the rain squall numbs to the bone.

I know these chaotic rocks flung pile-high
in cataclysms long since past. I follow where
the obliterated paths remember my aching feet.
Though I groan and weep aloud, I belong here.

It is true I have pleaded to be led
to some other country where the benign sun
kisses the unshielded brow, where the tear-spent face
is fingered by tender peace, and happiness is won.

But these my petitions plunge like bruised birds
to die in a ditch. This cursed kingdom is my share.
Hunger and thirst, weariness and loss—yet still I cry
"Praise God!" My half-demented wandering is my prayer.

Take my sad songs then—they tell of what I know.
Can the traveller report on undiscovered lands?
I stay where the justice of God has placed me
though my hot tears fall fast upon my folded hands.

6 Excavators and Passivity

To ENTER ANY of the nights of the soul is to continue in it till death. The night of faith remains with us in varying intensities because God can be approached in this life only through faith.

The active nights of sense and spirit persist because no matter how holy we become, we can still be tempted, concupiscence remains within us and must be countered, virtues can always be further perfected, involuntary imperfections show up and have to be overcome. Above all, we can always grow in love, and for this our own active efforts and self-denials are needed. They are also needed to keep the will in a state of passive openness to and acceptance of what God sends in the passive purgations.

The passive nights continue till that last moment of supreme passivity, death—and after, if we have not completed our purgatory here on earth.

God goes on working in our souls at ever deeper levels even in the state of transforming union. As long as we are on this side of death, the heavenly marriage can be perfected each day, just as an earthly one can. The more complete our abandonment in our passivity, the closer God embraces us in our inner selves, penetrating further as we yield up newly discovered tendencies of self-love and self-will.

Till we die we must work in and endure all the nights. Total rest and the completion of our work and God's within us comes only after death. For most, the deeper passive purgations will come only then too. For the few, they are completed in this life.

In the passive nights it is most important not to fight God's invasion. Resistance creates tension and distress, thus prolonging the cleansing process. Our chief and constant prayer must be the willed offering of our depths to God's secret action.

He is working to dredge up what needs purifying, his performance rather like that of a soundless excavator, throwing up rubble as it goes along.

This is the original clay and mud out of which he made humankind—the primeval sludge of evolution symbolically present in the buried recesses of the psyche. God means to locate and expose it so he can breathe his Spirit into it.

He says, "Let me act. Be still. Don't struggle. Don't have any of your own ideas about how this excavation should proceed. Just leave it to me and trust in the midst of absurdity."

In the passive purgations God is working to produce a state of total dependence. He wants us to be spiritual infants in his arms. We hurt because our self-will still strives to be in control of our lives, and we struggle to evade God's embrace, which only makes him hold us tighter.

He is teaching us, not by words or clearly understood concepts, but by stamping the seal of his grace upon our deepest selves—"God was here." Where he passes there is pain, but afterward comes peace and healing.

Just as the surgeon probes the secret recesses of the body, so the psychotherapist investigates those of the mind. No human therapist, whatever his skill and qualifications, can approach the Spirit's genius in this field. The following may help to give an idea of the depths at which the Spirit operates in our human psyches in the passive purgations.

Sometimes in a deep cutting for a road, or where a hillside has slipped away, or in such geological marvels as the Great Rift of Africa, the way the land has been built up is graphically revealed. Exposed are layer upon layer of differently colored and composed strata, sometimes in a regular pattern, sometimes twisted and whirled about by immense pressures and subterranean adjustments of the earth's surface.

The analogy is enriched if we imagine our layer system to be the exposed site of one of the chasms under the ocean—the Tuscarora Deep or the Marianas Trench. Not far down in the water perpetual night is reached, and in it swim terrifying monsters of the deep that have strange, built-in lighting systems of their own to entice and help them prey on other fish—a metaphor for the repressions and complexes that can, from the unconscious depths of the psyche, exert a devastating influence on our conscious areas of living.

These monsters too have to be tamed and brought under control by the Spirit. At the bottom, the trench's walls merge with the sea-bed. We might think of this as the ground of our being in which the mysterious presence of God abides, the alpha and omega, opening us to eternity and infinity. In psychological terms it could also be Jung's collective unconscious—the ultimate oneness of the human race, the hidden interconnectedness of all human beings, and maybe of all creation, taking place in God. Jesus sanctified all these areas by entering into them through his incarnation, for God is striving to express himself through our total being, sometimes using the unconscious elements, sometimes being fiercely opposed by them.

It is a fundamental truth of the spiritual life that grace builds on and perfects nature. Like a thrifty householder, the Spirit uses what is already there in his work of our sanctification. This includes the whole content of our inner selves down to the deepest elements in the unconscious, deriving perhaps from our life in the womb and forcible ejection in birth from its warm, amniotic enclosure.

The deepest of the passive purgations in the night of the spirit reach down into the fastnesses of this buried life to work upon the matter hidden there that is compulsively resisting grace's purifying action.

Usually the upper layers of the soul are penetrated first by grace, though sometimes God seems to take a random sample of the deeps, much as oil exploration teams do of what is below the ocean floor or the earth's crust.

Whatever form grace's exploration of and action upon our soul takes, complete passivity on our part can both ease and shorten the painful experience.

All these analogies and metaphors illustrate the activity of the agent and the necessary passivity of the recipient.

According to traditional teaching, these purifications occur at periods of transition in the spiritual life. The passive night of sense leads from meditation to contemplation, from the purgative to the illuminative way. The passive night of spirit occurs in the passage from simple contemplation to full union, while the soul is progressing from the illuminative to the unitive way.

In effect, such neat divisions are artificial, following only a general guide, for God's purifying action conforms to no specific rules or gradations, being adapted to each individual according to his or her needs and life circumstances.

Passive Purgations

Being a versatile excavator, water-diviner,
well-digger, underground-caver,
and subterranean explorer for hidden veins of gold—
not to mention master of the earthquake,
tsunami, volcanic eruption, and boiling mud pool,
being, as I say, expert in all these fields,
geological, marine, volcanological, metallurgical—
being all these plus the innumerable others—
being . . . well, he began, of course,
from two directions at once.

It was obvious to me, fearful though I felt,
that his method was indeed the most expeditious
to achieve his end, expose and clear away
all the relics, debris, danger areas and hidden traps
accumulated through millennia of laying down strata.

Still . . . being in the center of this waste-disposal unit
provoking ominous upheavals in my depths
while at the same time it ferociously attacked
and burrowed into every familiar hollow and protuberance
of what to me had been my terra firma on the surface—
though, of course, I always knew this was delusion
for the whole place was unstable, prone without warning
to convulsions, landslides, cave-ins, floods, and various other
cataclysmic reorganizations
such as children make with sand castles,
(even leaping into the middle of them) . . .
being, in fact, the subject of all this,
the very existential, blood, bone and wincing organism
it was his aim to redefine, reorientate, and purge drastically—
well . . . to put it briefly

I did not enjoy the procedure in any of its stages.

But
when it was all over and the veins of gold exposed
and the crater he had dug filled to the brim
with living waters shimmering in a soft, warm wind
and all my reshaped landforms gay with trees of life
and field flowers fluttering in the breeze—
well, then I did enjoy myself.
I did indeed.

7 I Am, Me and Eve

THERE IS EMBEDDED in human nature an unredeemed, primitive element that constantly chants, *I am. I want. Fulfill me.* It is embedded so deeply that it is hidden and rooted in the unconscious. It expresses itself through instinctual drives, overwhelming urges and irrational outbursts of passion that often disregard commonsense, duty and moral judgment. It operates separately from reason, intellect and acquired knowledge.

Let us call this primal urge simply ME. This suggests its supreme egoism and self-seeking nature.

It is, in fact, that aspect of human nature enmeshed in the first syndrome and called by Paul "the unspiritual." It is ruled by self-indulgence, some of its fruits being "depravity, rottenness, greed and malice . . . envy, murder, wrangling, treachery and spite" (Rom 1:29).

This ultimate ME claims the right to a self-subsistence only God possesses. ME declines to serve. It continuously makes a stubborn, rebellious, self-centered, ungraced, this-worldly affirmation of autonomy, acknowledging no creatureliness owing obedience to a Creator. In short, its rule of life is to do what will satisfy and gratify ME.

There is a spiritual force opposed to the ME. It is the divine I AM. The human mind cannot encompass the I AM is-ness of God. We can understand and accept that God created. That is an event in time, no matter how many aeons ago. We can understand and accept that in the fullness of time God sent his Son among us, for that too is an event in time, and even historically recorded.

We can understand and accept that at death we ourselves shall enter into eternity and infinity, for our death, too, is an event in time, and we have learned to surround what comes after with myth and symbol such as the Book of Revelation provides. These have a

61

comfortable aura of familiarity, keeping us within our own space-time continuum.

Of course, "understand" in the above contexts is relative. We think we understand, because this provides us with a sense of security that facing the fact of impenetrable mystery does not. But when we try to go back beyond the initial creation of all that is, and grasp what is meant by the eternal is-ness of God, our computer, baffled, breaks down.

Jesus said, "Before Abraham was, I AM," thus confronting us with the eternal Godhead.

God said to Moses, "I AM who I AM. . . . This is what you must say to the sons of Israel: 'I AM has sent me to you'" (Ex 3:14).

God also proclaimed himself as "the God of your fathers, the God of Abraham, the God of Isaac, the God of Jacob" (Ex 3:15), thus inserting himself into time and history on our level, so that in our limited way, we could grasp the fact of his being and presence among us and relate to him.

Scripture juxtaposes Christ and Adam, again associating in our minds the temporal and the eternal and their interaction. Of course the supreme, compelling interaction occurred in the incarnation itself. God became man and dwelt among us.

Juxtaposition occurs at the deepest level and central core of our own beings. Here the I AM of the Trinity present within us meets up with the I AM of our rebellious human identity whose basic drive is for self-realization in indifference to obedience to the divine will. Our I AM is one with the scriptural Adam after the fall—or Eve, since I am a woman.

Paul's unspiritual people are those in whom the Eve/Adam has never been graced. Their inner I AM is not qualified by any conception of God's I AM, or any impulse to worship and obey anything but its own existence and desires.

When these "unspirituals" become converted and begin to be swayed by the Spirit within, a conflict develops in them. Their ME becomes two-faced. It is partly graced and partly ungraced. Christ is intermittently active in their lives. They are at times under the control of the Spirit; they have a spasmodic desire to serve God and a hazy notion of what is entailed in this. However, the ungraced ME is still determinedly going its own way in them, and to a large extent their lives are shaped by its drive to fulfill itself at any cost.

In the more graced soul that Paul calls the "spiritual," motives and activity are more often than not aimed at pleasing God, following the Spirit's guidance and expressing the inward Christ-life outward upon others.

The I AM of God is deliberately opposed to the primitive, completely self-centered I AM. There exists in us the state of disruption that Paul bemoans, after observing it in himself (Rom 7:14-25). This is the usual state of the Christian in this life as he or she struggles to subdue the old man, the Adam/Eve, and bring to maturity the new man/woman, the Christed self.

"You cannot belong to Christ Jesus unless you crucify all self-indulgent passions and desires. Since the Spirit is our life, let us be directed by the Spirit" (Gal 5:24-25).

After years of struggle there may come a time when the primitive ME is under control as far as willful, outward expression of its impulses is concerned. There is a marked degree of inner peace. Virtues are well-established and habitually in evidence. We have an awareness of God present and active in our lives and are ruled by the desire to do his will and please him. We practice a simplified prayer, a low voltage contemplation.

We have become "spiritual."

"People who are interested only in unspiritual things can never be pleasing to God. Your interests, however, are not in the unspiritual, but in the spiritual, since the Spirit of God has made his home in you" (Rom 8:8-9).

The ME seems asleep, or even dead.

In John of the Cross terms, we have come through the night of sense and experience our inner house as being "at rest" because we are so deeply at peace and resting in the I AM of God, though we do not realize that this has come about only on one level of our being. We even imagine we have completed our spiritual training, and all we have to do now is remain in this peace.

But the primitive ME, though quiescent, is certainly not dead. It has merely withdrawn into a dark cavern in our inner abyss, waiting for the time to come when it will emerge to make a final and definitive assault to establish its supremacy. There is in us an inner core that still retains inviolate the primal assertion I AM in opposition to God's everlasting proclamation of sovereignty, "I AM the alpha and the omega; you are my created emanations."

We cannot, unaided, reach or unearth our own I AM at the depth it has buried itself. It still influences our behavior and attitudes, but we are blind to the nature and extent of its activities.

It is coterminous with our inner Eve who is ungraced, un-Christed, brooding in the darkness, primitive, elemental, tyrannical, passionate, irrational, intuitive, capricious, willful, possessed by a fierce creative urge that has become warped, potentially a powerhouse of energy to vitalize the spiritual, but too often permitting a dark, demonic force to utilize that energy in destructive, negative ways.

She is not evil herself, for God made her and all he made is good. But she is out of control, as it were, living her own often frenzied life there in the cave, submitting to no one (let alone Adam!), intent on getting her own way and ready to employ any means to that end. She has much in common with Freud's id, Jung's shadow, Harris' child.

There is only one person who can tame her and win her obedience, and that is the second Adam, Christ. Only he can transmute her vast, urgent energies so that she becomes "God's work of art, created in Christ Jesus to live the good life as from the beginning he had meant us to live it" (Eph 2:10).

Though she does not know it, this is what she is pining for—the Promised One who will invade her shadowy sanctuary, show her the beauty of the eternal I AM, and capture her allegiance and love.

In other words, Christ yearns after the unredeemed Eve/Adam in each one of us. The whole person has to be sanctified before being admitted to the wedding feast of the Lamb. God made us for himself, and he does not intend Eve to evade him forever. If she will not submit to being tamed in this life, she will have to in purgatory in the next. She must face facts at some stage, though primordial dreams of power are more in her line. The basic fact about her is that, all unknowingly, she herself is yearning for Christ, just as he yearns for her. In order to be graced, she must be lured from her hiding place and brought into consciousness.

There are therapeutic techniques for doing this. Having undergone psychoanalysis myself in my 20s, I know what a powerful help in the spiritual life the self-knowledge gained in such processes can be. They can also be harmful in the wrong hands.

The principal gains to me were (a) a willingness to face and ac-

knowledge the contents of my unconscious, especially the unruly
sexual elements; (b) a cleansing in some degree, of neurotic guilt;
(c) the reinforcement and deepening of a self-honesty already there;
(d) a deep self-acceptance; and (e) familiarity with techniques that
I myself could continue to use to bring about a deeper awareness
and constructive change in myself.

My experience of analysis as a vast eruption into consciousness
of emotions long repressed prepared me for later events in my spiritual life. When I became a Catholic in my late 30s and for the first
time discovered the depth and width of teaching on the doctrine
and practice of the spiritual life, I quickly saw the many links between this and all that I had studied and experienced in the field of
depth psychology. I set about, and have continued, relating the two
together.

Today they are freely interrelated by numbers of writers on the
interior life, but in 1956 this was not so. However I did discover a
few writers who dealt with the two together. Of especial help and
enlightenment was the Carmelite, Father Marie-Eugene's two vol-
umes on Carmelite spirituality. In the second of these, *I Am a
Daughter of the Church*, there is an excellent section on the similar-
ity of certain neurotic and psychotic states to those endured during
the passive purgations of the second night.

I acquired this book in 1957 and have, over the years, returned
to it again and again. Here I record my agreement with the author's
statement that "the purification of the spirit brings to the surface
with a painful awareness these (pathological and other) tendencies
deeply rooted in the faculties" (p. 356). They "come to the surface
and stand out in such relief during the dark night, only because they
are in eruption" (p. 359).

God is the prime mover in this eruption when it is a work of
grace and not merely a matter of psychotherapeutic technique with
a person who does not live in the faith dimension and is not experiencing the passive night.

Our role is to let the eruption happen in God's way and God's
time, submitting passively to the process and cooperating with our
will's full consent. Let no one imagine such passivity is easy. We
shall find adhering to it the most difficult and painful program of
our whole life.

Before the eruption began, or in the days of its earliest warning rumblings, we ourselves had already sensed there was a part of us, a hidden depth, not yet penetrated by the Spirit. Because we had reached the stage of genuinely longing to be possessed by God, we had begun to invite, implicitly if not explicitly, the Spirit's more complete upwelling.

At the same time God himself had decided we were ready for a more profound union with him. He began to draw our attention, probably only intuitively, to the existence of Eve and her need to be reborn in Christ.

Possibly a third thing happened. Eve herself became troubled by a mute yearning of a different quality from her usual primitive urges and desires. Something in her began praying, using only those untranslatable groanings that the Spirit utters when he prays within us. The essence of this primordial groan of longing is the closing invocation of the bible: "Come, Lord Jesus. Maranatha."

Now it is time for Jesus, answering her, to say, as to Lazarus, "Eve, come forth." But before she is discovered, revealed, clothed anew, and summoned to the wedding feast, an immense reorientation and transmutation of her powers has to come about.

God begins to turn his searchlight on Eve, there in her cavern of darkness, and she cannot escape. She is naked and cannot hide anything from the Spirit's ever-open eye that always discerns the exact truth. The Spirit is going to clothe her in the garment of grace ordained for her before ever she came into being, but for a long time this garment is going to feel to her like Eliot's "intolerable shirt of flame."

She will shriek in protest. She will try to fight off the Spirit. She will rush into the deeper recesses of the cave in an attempt to escape. She will call out "Yes! No!" and "No! Yes!" as she is torn between trust and terror. She will scream, "Go away and never come back!" and she will cry out in longing, "Come closer. I want you to possess me!"

Poor Eve! She will suffer as never before. And we, as we realize more and more fully that "Eve is ME . . . Eve is me," will suffer the same conflicts and terrors that she does.

There is much wisdom of a non-intellectual kind mixed up in Eve's wayward nature. We need to get in touch with it and have it blessed by divine Wisdom herself. We need to learn how to recognize and make right use of the wisdom she presents. Her emotional eruptions have to happen if our house is to be put in order and filled finally with peace. It is going to be hard for us to let these eruptions occur, acknowledge their content, be honest about them, and yet not identify with them.

The night of the spirit is much concerned with the purification of the emotions and what John calls "the passions of joy, hope, fear and grief." The night cleanses these of desires for and attachment to what is created and relates them to the Creator through whom they then return to creatures, spiritualized, in due proportion and intensity and freed from all self-seeking.

Eve has a long way to go before she can reach this state where her willful *I am, I want, fulfill me* gives way graciously and gladly to God's mighty I AM acting freely through her. And we have a long way to travel with her, not fighting and repudiating her, but helping and supporting her as an acknowledged, essential, valued part of us, and potentially, with her primal energy and instinctive wisdom, a most powerful ally in reaching the summit of the Mount of Perfection.

Eve and the Visitors

Eve
what are you doing down there in your cave?
I hear far sounds of commotion and my floor
is vibrating as if a subterranean tremor
was precipitating an earthquake.

Eve
I don't want any trouble from you just now.
I've recently put my house in order (though I admit

I had some help—from high up, I'd like you to know)
and I'll be really annoyed if you mess it up again.

Eve
I like it how it is now. It's feminine without being frilly,
it's restful without being soporific, it's shining clean
and fit for visitors at last. In fact, I'm entertaining
three of them. I hope you aren't going to disturb us.

Eve
if I let you come and join us will you behave yourself?
Here, take my hand. I can see you there, peeping
round the entrance to your cave. Come now,
put on your grass girdle, push the hair out of your eyes.

Eve
if you'll be a good girl, you can come. I know
you're longing to. Hush now. Tread gently. Don't speak.
Just sit down here on the floor at the feet of this one.
See, he's smiling at you. He wants to put his hands on your head
    to bless you.

Eve
be quiet and let him do it. There's nothing to fear.
Can't you feel how much he loves you? Dear Eve—my sister,
Eve, there's no need to cry and hide your face. He's smiling at you.
    Look.
He's speaking to you now. "Eve, welcome. I'm so glad you've
    come."

8 Log of Wood

In Book II, Chapter X, of *Dark Night of the Soul*, John of the Cross gives a useful summary of the progress of the passive purgations into the inner depths of our souls, using as an analogy the gradual penetration of fire into the heart of a log of wood.

He tells of how the soul (the log), once completely permeated by divine life (the fire), enters the supernatural state of transforming union, or spiritual marriage (log and fire become one, the log taking over the properties of fire). This state is what God intends as the destiny and final end of every human being, yet most regard it, if they even realize its existence, as some incredible condition to be found only in canonized saints. They do not link it up with contemporary emphasis on inner renewal, nor realize that John's teaching is applicable to themselves as they strive to express Christ's love in and for the modern world.

"The divine fire of contemplative love" that is purifying us is itself completely holy, pure, benign and beautiful, while we are tainted by "evil and vicious humours which the soul has never perceived because they have been so deeply rooted and grounded in it; it has never realized, in fact, that it has had so much evil within itself" (par. 2). Using the subject matter of the preceding chapter, we could say it has not faced up to its Eve/Adam.

These humors are what we would now name as the various psychological aberrations and aggravated or comparatively harmless tendencies which have been shaping our motives, attitudes and conduct in ways we have not realized. They have whipped up prejudices and misplaced ardors, while corrupting our human relationships with various hard-to-define but certainly evil influences of self-love and self-will.

To see all this, even out of the corner of one's eye, as it were, is alarming. We are lucky if we have an understanding, wise confes-

sor/director to support us as we face up to the truth. If not, we have
to apply an extra degree of trust and self-abandonment to divine
providence and accept the Spirit as our guide. He will certainly perform his role more than adequately if we do not close ourselves off
from him and retire into a welter of activities and distractions.

Although we usually remain rational enough to see that these
"evil and vicious humours," plus their effects, are not sins as such,
to recognize and accept their presence in ourselves constitutes a
moral shock. We are not deliberately sinning. In fact, after years of
struggle and mortification, deliberate sin has been excised from our
lives. Yet, deep in us is revealed "sin" itself.

What we see, of course, is original sin and its consequence, concupiscence. "As (the soul) sees in itself that which it saw not before,
it is clear to it that not only is it unfit to be seen by God, but deserves
his abhorrence, and that he does indeed abhor it" (par. 2).

Of course God continues to love us in spite of, and even because
of everything. What we experience is the impossibility of absolute
purity, beauty and holiness merging with or even touching impurity, ugliness and evil. As John emphasizes, "two contraries" cannot
mix and merge. This is the state of the log of wood at the beginning,
when it is first cast into the fire and the fire's effect is to make it seem
even blacker, darker and dirtier, in contrast to its own glorious in-
candescence. The log has not yet caught fire. It is first blackened by
smoke and heat and then has to be dried out before it will burn.

John calls the fire variously: purgative and loving knowledge;
divine light; mystical theology; divine fire of contemplative love;
loving wisdom; divine purgation; dark light of divine contemplation.

These titles taken together clearly convey that this purgative
activity comes from and is controlled by God. It is mystical and contemplative, being a grace received directly from God, by means of
which knowledge of how we appear in his sight is infused into us.
This wisdom is not something we could ever reach by natural reason or even the deepest ponderings. It has to be given. It can be
given only to those who are receptive.

Humble receptivity and a consuming hunger to be one with the
divine are absolute prerequisites for the infusion of these graces.

Having made his analogy, John develops it throughout the rest
of the chapter in a brief exposition of each of seven major points.

1) The fire of God's purgative love that reveals, excises and disposes of those evil roots underlying our surface behavior is felt by us as painful and destructive. Yet it is the same love that we shall later experience as "light" and as "loving wisdom," permeating us with the tenderest, most solicitous care once it has annihilated our dross.

2) We feel that God, or Wisdom, is punishing and repelling us. This, of course, cannot be true since God is love and his only action is one of infinite and eternal love.

What we are, in fact, experiencing, is the affliction of seeing ourselves exactly as we are in all our misery, weakness and wickedness. We had probably assessed ourselves as having reached a reasonable degree of sanctity. It is highly unpleasant to become aware that we have scarcely begun on the purgative way, and it is only human to transfer the blame rather than accept it ourselves. After all, the human race began doing this in Eden and has gone on ever since compulsively deflecting blame either onto God or someone else—anyone and anywhere as long as I can continue to view myself as praiseworthy and in the right.

This struggle to face up to one's real self has to take place, and the blame has to be accepted and absorbed, before we can begin to be sure from experience that the purgative fire is one of "divine light, sweetness and delight" (par. 4). In the meantime, it remains "afflictive." The soul is dark and troubled just as is the unlit log of wood until it is dried out and so prepared to receive the flame.

3) These afflictions are the same as those suffered in purgatory. It is fire which is commonly referred to in describing the sufferings of both purgatory and hell, the only difference between the two states being that one will be terminated and the other is everlasting. It is part of John's genius for describing the spiritual life that he uses the metaphor of fire for both the purgative process and the state of transforming union in "the living flame of love." Often the impression is given that the fire expresses God's revenge, hatred, rejection and repugnance—all these being vindictively directed toward the sinner.

Old style mission preachers would revel in descriptions of appalling torments, physical and spiritual, that left no doubt that God was a kind of sadistic torturer. Nuns and brothers used alleviated versions to control naughty children in the classroom, permanently damaging their psyches and their relationship with God in the process. That was the fashion. But it was theologically inexact.

The fire, whether directed on the soul of a saint on earth or in heaven, or that of a sinner on earth, in purgatory or in hell, remains the fire of God's *love*. It causes suffering when there is sin present, only because of the collision between the contraries of God's perfections and our imperfections. The big bang occurs in our psyches with resultant shock waves and even cataclysmic earthquakes.

"For the fire would have no power over them, even though they came into contact with it, if they had no imperfections for which to suffer" (par. 5).

God is never anything but perfect, everlasting love. He confronts sin with love, and sin, realizing at last its own nature, recoils in horror. In purgatory it offers itself to God to be cleansed, no matter how much it hurts, and eventually the hurt fades away into bliss. In hell it continues to shriek, "I will not serve!" and the hurt remains permanently.

"When the imperfections are consumed, the affliction of the soul ceases and its fruition remains" (par. 5).

The fruition, of course, is union in transforming love with the Trinity.

4) While the purification is taking effect, love grows more and more insistent in us as God pours his largesse into the spaces cleared by his own grace for his entry.

"Enkindling of love" is a phrase John often uses in relation to the infusion of grace into the soul. It vividly recalls the image of the log of wood, now well alight and beginning to flame. Once God begins to draw us into the union of love, the enkindling process of his love goes on uninterruptedly, providing we do not deliberately sin. However we do not necessarily feel any delight or warmth in love, for the reality of grace's presence and influence may well be concealed by the pain of the "dark contemplation" assailing us with that other truth about our helplessness and sinfulness.

When he judges it necessary for our encouragement, or right for the just balancing of truths, the Spirit reveals "the work that is being wrought in (the soul)" (par. 6) in its positive, consoling aspect. It is almost as if God takes from the furnace the iron he is working on to give us a chance to have a look and see that change has indeed taken place.

"There is a season for everything, a time for every occupation under heaven:

> A time for giving birth,
> a time for dying;
> a time for planting,
> a time for uprooting what has been planted.
> A time for killing,
> a time for healing;
> a time for knocking down,
> a time for building" (Eccl 3:1-3).

The Spirit alone can perfectly assess which season it is to be with us, and which is the appropriate activity. He is to be trusted and obeyed. We face and accept what is revealed to us whether it is shameful or consoling.

5) The pattern of purgation is cyclic. "After each of these periods of relief the soul suffers once again, more intensely and keenly than before" (par.7).

All the time the flame is penetrating farther into the log. This represents God's purgative action striking deeper in us around our roots, so that we may be "purified more inwardly" in a manner "more intimate, subtle and spiritual" (par.7).

What is "intimate" is related to our deepest and most private secrets and concerns. An intimate friend knows us very well indeed, receives all our confidences, and takes a personal, searching interest in our lives and our way of living them.

What is "subtle" is delicate, precise, dealing in the finer points, able to discern and differentiate accurately, perceptive in a piercing yet considerate manner, having discretion and sensitivity so that it can take all things into consideration while keeping them in perfect balance.

What is "spiritual" is to do with that immortal part of us that survives death and enters eternity. Obviously it is enduring and crucial in importance in a way that what is to do with the senses and emotions cannot be. Book II of *Dark Night* is to do with the purifying of this spiritual aspect of our being. It is a far more refined, penetrating work than that of the purgation of the senses. It is also a much more secret one.

The finesse required is possessed only by the Holy Spirit himself who "reaches the depths of everything, even the depths of God. . . .

Now instead of the spirit of the world, we have received the Spirit that comes from God, to teach us to understand the gifts that he has given us" (1 Cor 2:10, 12).

The fire is now refining those "spiritual imperfections . . . which are most deeply rooted in (our) inmost parts" (par. 7). In order to accomplish and complete its work it "acts with more force and vehemence in preparing (this) most inward part to possess it" (par.7).

The more forceful and even violent a penetration is, the more that which is being penetrated is likely to be broken to bits unless it relaxes and submits completely.

Perhaps John Donne had in mind the Spirit's "force and vehemence" acting to repel sin, when he implored God to "batter my heart . . . and bend/ Your force, to breake, blowe, burn and make me new" (Holy Sonnet XIV).

Donne accurately understood the need for inner renewal of a radical kind, and for purgatory endured, if not in this life, then after it, before God could be encountered.

He concludes this powerful sonnet, in which he encapsulates so much truth in metaphors of capture, by the startling paradox:

> Take mee to you, imprison mee, for I
> Except you enthrall mee, never shall be free,
> Nor ever chast, except you ravish mee.

The idea of being ravished by the Holy Spirit, being penetrated to one's "most inward (spiritual) part to possess it," horrifies and frightens the lukewarm and mediocre. To the ardent lover of God, who hungers and thirsts for him day and night, it is a call to surrender everything in order to receive all.

Scripture tells us that the kingdom of heaven is taken by force, and also that it is within us. When the Lord wants to take possession of this kingdom of his within us, he must use force if we refuse to cooperate. If we persist in trying to resist or even escape, he withdraws. By our fears and refusal to cooperate, we have chosen to endure our purgatory not now, but after death.

6) We see ourselves, in contrast to the pure blaze of the fire, as "full of evil" and this causes "bitterness" (par. 8) in us, for it is indeed bitter, after all our efforts, to see only darkness and sin, where we had hoped to find Christ enthroned in light and love.

We are like the log of wood that is now immersed in "consuming fire" so that no air reaches it. We stifle in our bitter helplessness, unable to believe our purgation is nearly accomplished.

Yet here, too, God usually grants periods of relief, when, our vision sharpened by what we have been through, and under the influence of Wisdom's discernment we see that darkness and sin in us are not the final reality. Light and holiness are, and the Spirit has already won over large sections of our foundation self and infused his purity into them.

(7) Near the end of the purifications joy may be so "ample" that we imagine our sufferings have ended and we have attained the goal of transformation in love. At the same time a niggling warning tells us that more is in store for us, "a new assault seems to be threatening" because, out of the corner of our eye, as it were, we glimpse the "root of imperfection which remains" (par. 9).

No one can enter God's presence without being totally clothed in the wedding garment of grace given by him out of his infinite mercy. We have to "put on Christ"—or, rather, in terms of the passive purgations, we have to permit Christ to put himself into us. The old man must be replaced by the new man grace has fashioned.

We must have received the "stone with a new name written on it, known only to the man who receives it" (Rev 2:17); to have "washed [our] robes white again in the blood of the Lamb" (7:14); to have the Lamb's "name and his Father's name written on [our] foreheads" (14:1).

All this means that we must be not only chosen by God, but we must deliberately choose him ourselves. We must be not only clothed outwardly in a wedding garment, but have it so drenched in the sacrificial blood of Christ, with which we have mingled our own, that our inner beings have the white purity of perfect love. We must not only be openly named and called by the Father as his, but have willingly given up our secret selves to his love's invasion to the point of ravishment.

"It is the most inward part that remains longest unkindled" (par.9) both in our own depths and in the log's center.

With this light given us by the Spirit we can now clearly see the difference between this area of darkness and the light- and grace-filled spaces around it. It remains there obstinately, a bit like a pile of dirt swept under the carpet that we hope no one will notice.

However, under the Spirit's vigilant guidance, we ourselves cannot avoid noticing it, and as soon as we do, we are consumed with longing to have it cleaned up so the Trinity can take total possession.

Grace progresses inward, as in Teresa's *Mansions*. The most interior sufferings are the most excruciating, yet having reached the stage of being almost there, we could not, and have no wish to turn back. Our one ruling desire is to be completely penetrated by this divine fire, at whatever cost to ourselves, and be with Christ forever.

Dying to Be Reborn

Death, they say, is easy.
At the end the passing over
comes peacefully. No agonies
no terrifying throes and struggles
to evade relinquishment.

I didn't find it so. For me
the spasms were prolonged and fierce,
limbs thrashed about in protest
rebellious breath fought to stay
functional in flaccid, enervated lungs.

For me it was not easy.
The urge to keep control, to cling
to what I cherished, to crush it to my breast,
fought with my will to yield to you.
You won. At last I bowed my head and died.

9 The Inflowing of God

The doctrine of the immanence and indwelling of the Trinity is scriptural, especially emphasized by Jesus at the Last Supper. It is also experiential, as any lover of the Lord can testify. That God is within the human heart is a fact the lover is certain of, though he or she cannot explain how or accurately locate the Presence.

God is also transcendent, "out there" in the sense that he permeates and keeps in being the whole of his creation. But for Christians living their faith daily and in all circumstances, the dynamic fact is that God is "in here." He is "with" us, he inhabits our deepest places, and his hallowing influence pervades us from that hidden sanctuary, for we truly are the temples of the living God.

Those to whom St. John of the Cross addresses his treatise on the night of the spirit already live in constant awareness of the mysterious, compelling, inner Presence.

In the log of wood analogy John presented God as gradually penetrating further and further from the periphery. We can think of "inflowing" in the same way, but if we accept that God is already present through grace in our inner depths, the ground of our being, then it is also true to think of the inflowing of God as an upwelling, like artesian waters, from a hidden source within our own inner fastness. His purpose is to permeate us from where baptism placed him, "here within."

The doctrine of the indwelling of the Trinity is one of the church's most spiritually compelling and fruitful. In his treatise on the dark night, John is examining the way in which this indwelling increases its power and presence till it accomplishes its will to possess us completely, to our own supreme fulfillment and final joy in the third syndrome of light-joy-fulfillment.

We were created to be receptacles of God, just as the ciborium is fashioned and used to hold the hosts and the chalice the wine.

"This dark night is an inflowing of God into the soul" (*D.N.* I,V,1). If we consider the infinite immensity of God and the apparent finiteness of our inner being, it seems impossible that such an inflowing could take place without either shattering us or sending us mad. In fact, if we resist, either of these alternatives is possible.

But if we recall that it is our spirit God invades, and that he himself is pure Spirit, and that spirits are, of their nature, immaterial and boundless, then a different perspective results. We can see that the process is like water flowing into water, yet we can touch, see, taste and even hold water in our cupped palms. We cannot do any of these with spirit.

"The spirit in the Old Testament, originally the wind and the breath, is conceived as a divine dynamic entity by which Yahweh accomplishes his ends: it saves, it is creative and charismatic power, and as an agent of his anger it is a demonic power. . . . Spirit is opposed not to the material (for which there is no Hebrew word) but to flesh—the mortal, corruptible, weak and sinful element in man. Spirit is not flesh" (McKenzie, *Dictionary of the Bible*, pp. 841-842).

In the New Testament, (see McKenzie, pp. 842-845), the concept of spirit is varied and greatly enriched. The spirit is the mysterious, saving power of God; the spirit authenticates Jesus as Messiah; the growth of the church is the work of the spirit; it empowers the disciples to be witnesses to the resurrection; it manifests itself through various charismatic phenomena; it is given to the whole body of believers; it is a divine, dynamic force.

In Paul's writings the spirit pervades Jesus and his mystical body, the church; the risen Lord exists in the spirit, not the flesh; the spirit frees from sin and death; it is the creative, life-giving force present in the risen Jesus and through him in the church; it makes them both the temple of its indwelling, praying in them, sanctifying them, distributing gifts, bestowing salvation.

The believer knows, understands, has faith, hope and charity, only through and in the spirit; it stands in antithesis to the flesh, which is both the law and the tendency to sin; there is in the believer a conflict between flesh and spirit, between the principle of corruption and of eternal life.

John's gospel stresses the spirit as Paraclete (helper) and spirit of truth; the words of Jesus, which are the revelation of God, are spirit and life; the spirit is streams of life for the believer; it enables the apostles to remove sin; it is sent by the Father, and by Jesus; it remains forever; it reveals the true reality of Jesus.

Pondering the above, we see how wide and deep is the Spirit's influence and power in the spiritual realm of our lives.

If we think of our inner integration as the work of the Holy Spirit, which it is, for he is the Sanctifier, we shall find it easier to disencumber ourselves from limiting concepts of time, space and ourselves as bodies of flesh destined for corruption. We shall gain a perspective in which eternity and infinity are seen as realities, and our spirits as immortal and therefore partaking of eternity and infinity now. The mystery of the inflowing of God into, or up through the soul, though not understandable intellectually, will become acceptable in faith.

The inflowing *can* happen. It *does* happen. By means of it, "God secretly teaches the soul and instructs it in perfection of love, without its doing anything, or understanding of what manner is this infused contemplation" (*D.N.* II,V,1).

The secrecy is because the divine action occurs in those deeply hidden recesses of the unconscious which our human understanding cannot reach, and in a way it cannot grasp. Spirit infuses divine love into spirit, which remains passively receptive, this receptivity being a positive act of our will to remain open to God no matter what. "Not doing anything" is, paradoxically, a concentrated willingness to "let God do." His doing comes about in a blind stirring of love in thick darkness. Why he does what he does, we cannot know. How he accomplishes his ends, we cannot understand.

All we can grasp is that God's action *is*. As contemplation deepens, this is-ness becomes a basic fact and experience in our spiritual life.

In the active nights we have already done all we could through our own deliberate efforts, aided by grace, to clear out of God's way all that could impede his inflowing. The rubbish gone and the channel opened, we have now to leave the regulation of the living waters to him. He will also deal with the embedded detritus still in places clogging the bed of the stream and the roots of the trees impeding the flow along its banks.

At times our spirit is able to receive the action and invasion of the divine Spirit in tranquillity. But mostly, John warns us, it experiences "affliction and torment."

The soul's state is like that of a foreigner in a strange land. He is an exile who will never be able to go home again, for all routes back have been blocked by a cataclysmic earthquake—the eruption of the divine into his inner depths.

Of course he suffers, at times atrociously. His only recourse is to submit and blindly trust.

It is "the height of Divine Wisdom, which transcends the talent of the soul" that causes it to suffer during this inflowing; as does also the growing awareness of "its (own) vileness and impurity" revealed in contrast to the beauty and purity of the enlightening Spirit (D.N. II,V,2).

So we have inability to comprehend on one level, coupled with an only too exact comprehension on another level. What a clash and discord! What war between "two contraries"!

"The natural strength of the intellect is transcended and overwhelmed by (this) great supernatural light" (D.N. II,V,3).

The impact of the collision of divine Sinlessness with human sinfulness produces other effects on our inner being that overflow into mind, emotions and body.

We feel enmity between ourselves and God as if there were a life and death battle going on, and we in imminent danger of being annihilated by a force as mighty as a nuclear holocaust. We feel fear, dread of destruction, pitiful longing to be spared. Peter cried, "Depart from me, O Lord, for I am a sinful man!" For the first time we truly experience Peter's dilemma and the full reality of being embedded in the fallen human race with no possible rescuer except the divine and sinless Savior.

To experience God as an implacable enemy, who crushes one underfoot while he gazes with merciless, all-seeing eyes upon the wreckage that was once our proud, inviolable, complacent selves, is truly to become frantic to flee.

The psalmist experienced the same dread and defeat:

> You have plunged me into the bottom of the pit, into
>   the dark abyss,
> Upon me your wrath lies heavy,

And with all your billows you overwhelm me. . . .
My only friend is darkness (Ps 87, Confraternity Version).

This is one of the passion psalms. It foretells the plight of Jesus dying on the cross under the fearsome load of the world's sin, and feeling even God had abandoned him because of the inevitable recoil of Sinlessness from what he had permitted himself to become immersed in by consenting to "become Sin for our sakes." In our own spiritual trial, Jesus on the cross is our refuge, and uniting our anguish with his is our way to sanity and hope.

God's purpose in letting his love for us register on us as dire enmity is to strip us of our hidden pride by showing us the truth about ourselves, that we are "unworthy of God or of any creature" (*D.N.* II,V,5). And we had thought ourselves well on the way to being canonized, and much further up the *nada* path than anyone we knew, or graciously compared ourselves with.

Now in our grim self-knowledge of our "evils and miseries," we cannot see how we can ever overcome or escape or be cleansed from them. God permits this experience of helplessness so that we shall have no other solution but to turn to his mercy and love, claiming in faith what he has promised us, "Come unto me all you who are heavy-laden, and I will refresh you."

The hand that smites is also the one that heals. In fact, the very smiting is an essential part of the healing process.

At other times when the inflowing is strong, we experience ourselves "as if beneath some immense and dark load" (*D.N.* II,V,6). This is because God's invasion has reached a degree of forcefulness that cannot be deflected. His presence is thrusting in upon us deep down in the ground of our being, and we are as yet too spiritually weak either to withstand or receive it.

This is the effect of what John calls "substantial touches." These are the caresses of Love registering directly upon the inner substance of the soul—Spirit to spirit. Until we have become other Christs in transforming union, we may experience such a divine touch as a kind of crushing under the heel of a giant.

"A thing of great wonder and pity is it that the soul's weakness and impurity should now be so great that, though the hand of God is of itself so light and gentle the soul should now feel it to be so heavy and so contrary, though it neither weighs it down nor rests upon it, but only touches it, and that mercifully, since he does this in order to grant the soul favours and not to chastise it" (*D.N.* II,V,7).

God's desire to possess our spirits completely is as importunate as any passionate lover's on the fleshly level.

Because this inflowing has passed far beyond the outer self and the senses and is thrusting in toward the furthest recesses of our being, the bottom of the inner abyss, the most secret, deepest strata of our psyches where no one has ever reached before, let alone touched us, we are both terrified and appalled.

If this can happen to us, anything can happen. There is no refuge left, nowhere to flee or to hide.

> Where could I go to escape your spirit?
> Where could I flee from your presence?
> If I climb the heavens, you are there,
> There too, if I lie in Sheol (Ps 139:7-8).

We are indeed in Sheol, and he is indeed there. And what is he doing? He is "stripping (us) of the habitual affections and attachments of the old man, to which (we are) very closely united, knit together and conformed" (*D.N.* II,VI,1).

"Affections and attachments" are the equivalent of addictions. An addiction is something or someone we are quite unable to give up through will power alone. Think of the alcoholic who is impotent against his hated addiction until he acknowledges his helplessness and deliberately submits to a Higher Power.

Think of the fanatically obsessed lovers who are ready to wreck others' lives and their own if only they can be together and satisfy their addiction. Their compulsion is a kind of emotional devouring of each other, yet they are convinced it is the noblest of loves, excusing the drastic betrayal of other loyalties, if only they can satisfy their mutual craving.

Or think of the workaholic, the sportaholic, the drug addict— anyone with a "magnificent" (or debasing) obsession or a compulsion to use others in some way or other while sincerely professing the most sublime of motives. Think of the do-or-die fanaticisms, the my-country-right-or-wrong blindnesses, together with the extensive, devious rationalizations twined around them like well-established, clinging ivy. Think of these only too common habitual mechanisms of human living, loving and being, and you have some idea of what John so accurately diagnoses to be there in our depths, running our lives for us.

They are all part of the "old man," the racial entity we are born into and cannot escape from except by grace, the first sin-suffering-evil syndrome clamped on us that only the second and third syndromes can dislodge.

"United, knit together, conformed. . . ."

We are one with this old man through both heredity (racial and personal) and environment. We are so much one with him that we are knit together. We can no more be unravelled from him and his influence than one colored wool thread can be abstracted from the pattern it makes with the other colors, without destroying the whole garment.

We are conformed to the old man within, molded by our immersion in humanity, so that we let him express himself as he wishes through us, using us to repeat his patterns over and over and over again. (Think of the repetitive patterns of world history, let alone those of the individual.)

Seeing all this by divine revelation, Paul cried out, "I do those things I don't want to do, and what I want to do, I don't do. Who will deliver me from the body of this death (the old man)?" He answered himself, "Nothing else but the grace of our Lord Jesus Christ!" (See Rom 7:14-25.)

Paul was enduring the inflowing of the ray of divine darkness revealing to him his human plight and his only remedy for it—the redeeming, renewing graces bestowed by Jesus through the penetration of his Spirit.

We are imprisoned in "this sepulchre of dark death (of the old man) . . . until the spiritual resurrection which we hope for" (*D.N.* II,VI,1).

We have to die on one level before we can be reborn on another. The grain of wheat has to fall into the ground and change radically or it cannot bear fruit.

"The sepulchre of dark death" is the place where we face both God and ourselves, and see the disparity. Because our faith, hope and love have already been purified to some degree by our earlier struggles and purgings, and contemplation has been established, though imperfectly, in us, we are able, even though in such sore straits, to cling to hope. As we are now so closely one with the suffering Lord and his death, we have, deep within us, the indestructible certainty that one day, when God is ready, we shall rise with him.

But before that, we must die with him, bcoming entirely passive and entombed, while Spirit works his miracle of transformation in us.

For J.B.K.—On the Ocean Bed

"On the ocean bed," you write, my friend . . .
Down in the unalleviated dark
where all those nightmare monsters of the deep
cruise and lurk, with dangling lights to lure
unwary prey into their gaping mouths.

I know the exact place where you are
because I've been there too.
                            The ooze
of endless ages makes a clammy couch.
No sun will ever penetrate this bathyal zone—
night here is total, its pervasive cold
enough to chill the very heart to death.

This rudimentary diving-suit enclosing you
provides a simple intravenous nourishment
for those immured in enforced passivity.
In some strange way it reassures you

you are cherished and sustained within
a mighty oceanic womb of love.

The loneliness and tedium are cruel.
The numbness makes an idiocy
of all endeavour. You idly turn and turn
in sluggish currents stirred up by
those fishy predators. Your brain
is addled. You had a purpose once
but what it was you scarcely can recall
much less now clarify and reaffirm.

The only course left open to you
is to wait . . . And so you wait . . .
invasion of your silence and your solitude
comes only from the gliding monsters' menace.
Their strange communications—whistles, grunts and squeals,
deep sonar booms and thuds, reverberate
about you in the fluid dark's immensity.

After what seems like centuries there rises
from some stubborn faith concealed beneath your drowned
disintegrating mind, a wordless message.
Gently surfacing, it formulates itself
upon a scarlet banner lit for you to read:

Those that meekly wait upon the Lord
content with drowning in his love
will surely see his face.

10 Circumcision of the Heart

Ascent, BOOK III explains what we ourselves are able to do by way of deliberate reordering of our inner selves to perfect our purity of loving intention. Chapters 16-23, which relate well to *Dark Night*, Book II, deal specifically with the active purgation of the will.

The theme is summarized in this sentence: "Moral good consists in the restraining of the passions and the curbing of disorderly desires, from which restraint there come to the soul tranquillity, peace and rest, and moral virtues" (*Ascent* III,V,1).

We can do much to stop memory dwelling obsessively on events and people that have stirred up our emotions so that we become unduly preoccupied with what was said, done and felt. In such a state we swing from one extreme to the other, have our judgment disturbed, are tossed about in emotional turmoil, and are distracted from prayerful recollection and inner contemplative stillness.

This is because the will (heart) is drawn forcefully toward, and desires to possess, what is not-God. The not-God includes the sweetness and delight we have had in our relationship with God, the memory of which makes us long to experience it again. If the will and imagination and memory cling to these, we are hindered from advancing in union with God himself through a deeper contemplative prayer.

Because these prayer experiences were more spiritual than those earlier ones which had much more of the senses and emotions in them, it is all the more dangerous to hanker after their consolation, for this invites delusion and provides an opening for the devil to deceive us about our relationship with God. We have at any time little capacity to understand the supernatural, and it is best not to try to, nor to dwell on its manifestations, but to leave such matters to God while we concentrate on doing his will.

The great danger in clinging to past experiences is the fostering of "a certain secret satisfaction . . . great spiritual pride . . . secret self-esteem . . . taking more delight in (our) own spirituality and spiritual gifts than those of others" (*Ascent* III,IX,1 & 2).

This, of course, is very similar to what we encountered in the "faults of beginners," where the passive purgations of sense were involved, only these faults of a higher stage of union are at a much deeper, more serious level, precisely because the soul is so much closer to God and most of the surface debris has already been disposed of.

The least act of humility, John assures us, is worth more than all visions, revelations and spiritual feelings, so do not dwell on them, covet them or hug them to you.

"It is good for the soul to desire to understand nothing, save God alone, through faith, in hope" (*Ascent* III,XIII,9). This means it is best to avoid all such ponderings as: What degree of prayer is this? Which stage of the spiritual life does that mean I'm in? Does that revelation mean I've received the gift of discernment? Am I a mystic? Is this contemplative prayer? What did God mean by that? Why doesn't he come to me like that again? Was that an ecstasy? It is best to tell one's director simply what happened, and then leave all judgments and labelling to him. If he is an expert, experienced director, he will probably be non-committal. This is crucifying to self-love and excellent for humility.

The title of this chapter recalls scriptural references to that inner, symbolic circumcision of a heart renouncing sin and self-love. A circumcised heart obeys God and accepts his laws and judgments out of love for him. Abraham was justified by faith, not by physical circumcision.

"The real circumcision is in the heart—something not of the letter but of the spirit" (Rom 2:29).

Circumcision according to Christ means being buried with him through baptism, and being raised up with him in faith and love by God's power. Being dead in sin is the equivalent of having an uncircumcised heart. The spiritual circumcision of baptism means metanoia, entry into the life of love in Christ, and the forgiveness of sins (See Col 2:11-13).

Jesus himself stressed the inwardness of sin and the absolute necessity of purity of heart. John of the Cross is following close after him. Purity of heart means for him detachment from the not-God and total attachment to and love of God and his will. This is exactly what Jesus taught.

"The strength of the soul consists in its faculties, passions and desires, all of which are governed by the will. Now when these faculties, passions and desires are directed by the will toward God, and turned away from all that is not God, then the strength of the soul is kept for God, and thus the soul is able to love God with all its strength" (*Ascent* III,XVI,2).

This is really about single-mindedness and steadiness of purpose. It is also a paraphrase of the supreme commandment to love God above all, and with all one's being (see Dt 6:5), which Jesus himself both confirmed and exemplified.

When faced with this summons to reckless self-giving, we make endless qualifications, excuses and rationalizations. John will have none of them.

Our hearts must be purged of all unruly affections and desires arising from the four traditional passions of joy, hope, fear and grief. When we calmly consider what and who does actually arouse in us the extremes of these passions, we shall not often find that it is our personal relationship with God.

John insists that, when these passions "are controlled by reason according to the way of God," we rejoice only in what is purely to do with the honor and glory of God, hope for only that, grieve only over what concerns it, and fear nothing but God himself and being separated from him. When our emotions and purpose for living are completely centered on God, it is obvious that "the strength and ability of the soul are being directed toward God and kept for him" (*Ascent* III,XVI,2).

The aim of this purging of desires for the not-God is to transform our human will into one fully united with the divine will. The more we are emotionally dependent on created things and on people, the more our will is tugging to get free of God, or is in conflict, or is merely ignoring the directives of his will for us.

If we succeed in fully controlling only one of the four passions, the others will also become subdued and redirected to God as a result. Until we achieve this control, we remain captive and incapable of full union and deep contemplation. Subject to these basic drives and emotions, we are unable "to remain in the tranquillity and peace which are necessary for the wisdom which, by natural or supernatural means, (we are) capable of receiving" (*Ascent* III,XVI,6).

It is the misdirection of "the affection of love" that is at the root of most of the trouble. This phrase in John's vocabulary means craving, addiction, obsession, dependence, attachment causing anxiety, urge for ownership, possessiveness, inordinate desire, strong ambition . . . . Since we are now in the night of spirit, these "affections of love" will be concerned with spiritual more than physical, sensible areas of our being and life.

If a person is attached strongly to the not-God, the result is that he "neither has nor possesses anything; it is rather they that have possessed his heart and he is, as it were, a sorrowing captive" troubled by disquietude and grief. In contrast, and by using a powerful metaphor, John teaches that "he that is detached is untroubled by anxieties, either in prayer or apart from it; and thus, without losing time, he readily gains great spiritual treasure. But the other man loses everything, *running to and fro upon the chain by which his heart is attached and bound*; and with all his diligence he can still hardly free himself for a short time from this bond of thought and rejoicing by which his heart is bound." What is the remedy? John replies, "The spiritual man, then, *must restrain the first motion of his heart towards creatures*" (*Ascent* III,XX,3).

Anyone who thinks this is easy is either (1) severely emotionally inhibited and repressed; (2) naturally unresponsive and coldhearted; (3) ignorant of what it is to love with all the too, too human heart; (4) a psychopath; or (5) already a saint!

John pushes home his point relentlessly. "There is another very great and important benefit in this detachment of the rejoicing from creatures—namely, that it leaves the heart free for God. This is the dispositive foundation of all the favours which God will grant to the soul, *and without this disposition he grants them not*" (*Ascent* III,XX,4, italics added).

John does not qualify the above statements. He never compromises regarding what God requires of us. He presents us with a clear directive of what to do, obviously convinced it is within our power, with the help of grace, to do it. This is a presupposition of the active night. We are able to will an action and then carry it out. We are thus "active" in helping ourselves to come closer to God.

But what if, in spite of repeated, sincere, whole-hearted (that is, as far as possible in our imperfect state) efforts, we still find we cannot subject "the affection of love" to reason and will? (Again, we are reminded of Paul in Romans 7.)

This is where the passive purgations come to our aid, and through patiently endured, God-imposed suffering, enable us to get free. Now God acts, God does, God wills, God subdues and eliminates. We passively submit and let God act, perhaps in one of the following ways, through circumstances we can neither control nor avoid:

- He removes us spatially far from the object of our desire, or it from us.

- He causes the person we love and itch to be close to, to spurn, renounce or cease to love us.

- He makes it impossible for us to fulfill ourselves in this particular way, whatever it is, by visiting upon us an accident, an illness, a physical or mental disability or decline, a disaster that destroys our financial resources, an unavoidable duty that forces us to change our ways and be continuously distracted from and unable to make contact with the object of our "affection of love."

Our addiction need not be a person. It could be an ambition (including the apparently laudable, spiritual one of becoming a saint). God may negate this ambition by making us lose all confidence in being able to operate in its field and attain our desired goal.

We may crave the fulfillment of a God-given skill and vocation to one of the arts or perhaps to guiding souls, and circumstances now make it impossible for us to exercise that skill or have contact with souls.

We may be wrapped up in a work obviously initiated by God for his church, and for a long time blessed with fruition, but then suddenly all our efforts are frustrated, and the work itself evaporates, all its fruits ruined.

The compulsive center of our life may be a happy, holy marriage dedicated to God and producing offspring also dedicated to God (one recalls St. Therese's family), but unexpectedly one partner is stricken with a terminal illness or killed in an accident, and the other is left to cope with inconsolable grief, and work through to heroic abandonment (as Therese's father certainly did).

Whatever it is, we personally and consciously do not do, or choose, or contrive the destroying, removing, negating, killing factor—it *happens*. If we have faith and trust, we know this mangling is divine providence at work out of a love that bewilderingly registers on us as hate.

And so we are in the world of paradoxes and ambiguities again. Our understanding is being smothered. Our heart is being circumcised, and indeed crucified and martyred. We are back with Jeremiah with his being a mark for God's arrows, with Hopkins' "lionlamb" pressing menacingly upon him, with the psalmist plunged into the bottom of the pit. We remember Hopkins' words:

> Thou art indeed just, Lord, if I contend
> With thee; but, sir, so what I plead is just.
> Why do sinners' ways prosper? and why must
> Disappointment all I endeavour end?
> Wert thou my enemy, O thou my friend,
> How wouldst thou worse, I wonder, than thou dost
> Defeat, thwart me? Oh, the sots and thralls of lust
> Do in spare hours more thrive than I that spend,
> Sir, life upon thy cause. . . .

The circumcision of the heart must become the heart's martyrdom and crucifixion in some way or other, if it is to attain final and complete subjection to God and become one with his will, so that all its joy, hope, fear and grief are concentrated upon his honor and glory.

Only when this happens can his life and love flow without obstruction into and through us for others. Then at last we can rejoice in what pleases him, hope for what will fulfill his purposes for creation, fear what will thwart these, grieve when sin flouts his declared command to love and confronts his perfect purity with the insult of an impure, other-directed heart.

The passive purgations of the spirit are concerned with what we do and are, in spite of ourselves, with what is unrelated or poorly related to God's honor and glory, and his will for our and others' sanctification.

To become saints we have to be at work all the time, passively if not actively. For most of us that is too much of an effort, a demand too absolute for us to meet, so we die unsanctified and have to be stripped of all those non-essentials in purgatory. Though we emerge wearing a wedding garment, it is a nondescript, pallid thing compared with the glorious, unique, bejewelled model God had intended for us if we had only let him circumcise our hearts during our lifetime in the way and to the degree he meant for us.

"For this is the will of God—your sanctification" (1 Thes 4:3).

John gives some infallible signs by which we can know our personal relationships express the love of a circumcised heart. Because it has struggled free of addiction (the "affection of love") and has no need to devour anyone emotionally or be devoured, this heart is now "free and able to love them all rationally and spiritually, as God wills them to be loved" (*Ascent* III,XXIII,1).

It is not snared, entranced and hypnotized by natural beauty, gifts, talents, personality, charm. It may appreciate and value these, but it does not fall in love with them.

Why?

Because at last it is totally and wholly in love with Love itself. Through the wisdom and discernment bestowed by the Spirit of Love, it understands that it is virtue, moral beauty, abandonment to God's will, gift of self to him that, present in another, compel and deserve love.

In a key passage John affirms that "when we love in this way, it is very pleasing to the will of God, and also brings great freedom; and if there be attachment in it, there is greater attachment to God. For, in that case, the more this love grows, the more grows our love toward God; and, the more grows our love toward God, the greater becomes our love for our neighbour, for, when love is grounded in God, the reason for all love is one and the same and the cause of all love is one and the same also" (*Ascent* III,XXIII,1).

The "reason and the cause" for such a pure and spiritual quality in human love is Love itself. Because we let him, Love has taken over our hearts in the passive purgations, and his power has set us free from compulsive appetite and emotional need. We no longer use the objects of our love for our own satisfaction and the fulfilling of our unconscious drives and needs. Instead, we reverence them as priceless gifts from God, to be loved with his love, for his sake, to his honor and glory, and to their blessedness. We have renounced the itch to possess the beloved emotionally and to get something for ourselves out of loving and being loved. This does not mean we receive nothing. In this blessed state, on the contrary, we receive riches and joy beyond what we even hoped for or dreamed longingly about. And these blessings are permanent, not unstable and transitory.

Instead of internal turmoil, entangled emotions, agitated fears and wants, and ephemeral rejoicing, we now experience interior peace because we are resting in God's will. He has chosen and given this personal relationship to us, we ourselves have not snatched, selected or hungered for it, except insofar as we longed to honor and glorify him through it, if that was his will.

Because we rest in his will with a circumcised heart that is pure, whole, free and recollected, we experience great tranquillity in the soul and freedom from distractions and the need to gaze avidly upon the beloved, thus indicating a captive heart.

Because the heart no longer "rejoices in natural graces and good things," it has become "a worthy temple of the Holy Spirit" and at last the Trinity can dwell undisturbed in it (*Ascent* III, XXX,4).

Falling in love with Love has been consummated in a much deeper union, and because we renounced everything for God, we have received it back a hundredfold but purified into heavenly beauty and holiness.

Eve Inside Her Cave at Night

Eve
you're fond of that primeval cave of yours
with all its runic drawings on the walls. In spite
of its deep-probing inner corridors and alcoves
no one penetrates for tingling dread
of awesome spirits brooding there, you love it.
It's home for you, my Eve, my sister Eve.

Eve
I watch your darting, fearful eyes interrogate
the shadowy clefts and slits the flickering flames
fill with menace. Your fire dramatizes
the roof's soaring vault lost in smoky gloom.
You know impenetrable dark envelops
those rock-bound arteries you would not dare to probe.

Eve
you lie there rigid on your animal furs
clutching their familiar hairiness about you
aware of other eyes beyond the cave-mouth fire
that glitter in the boundless, aboriginal night.
The prickling stars and slim gold curve of moon
do not dispel those predators' prowling threats.

Eve,
Mother Eve, your cave and you exist in me.
Come, still your fears. Someone you do not know
once journeyed into all our stygian Hades.
Each step he took was through your cave's
mysterious inner depths, and where he passed he shed
ineffable light that never fails. He left behind—

Eve
listen to me—he left there in your cave
a Spirit quite unlike those lurking foes
you tremble at. If you will only trust enough you'll see
how every passageway is noonday bright—
no crack or crevice left unlit.
                          A multitude
of votive lamps glow everywhere unquenchably.

11 Clinging and Whirling

THE TRANSITION FROM sense to spirit in the passive purgations is a severe shock to the whole human system. Subjectively it registers in various ways according to the individual's needs as Wisdom sees them. Two common ones are a sensation of being suspended in space, either clinging perilously to something, or being madly whirled about. The following analogies develop these two themes.

The feeling of being suspended psychologically and spiritually between heaven and earth produces a vertiginous kind of existence like that of a climber high up on a cliff face clutching at tiny protuberances because he knows that to let go means a fall to death.

This cliff face can simply be called God. As we ease ourselves higher up the Mount of Perfection—or are lifted there in Therese's divine elevator—we cling to this flinty surface that seems neither to yield nor to receive us in its indifference. While we hang there, suffering giddiness, fear and a sense of rejection, we continue to affirm, "This is the bosom of God, the warm nest of his love for me, the everlasting enfoldment of his tender arms." The senses mock at such a paradox, but faith holds fast.

In many of the psalms God is compared to a rock fastness, a place of high grandeur where we are safe from the enemy, an impregnable haven that endures and will endure throughout all tempests. Our comfort as we clamp ourselves precariously to this rocky cliff face is our faith that when we seem most in peril, we are, in fact, safest. God will not allow us to fall, though he does permit the terror of falling to shatter self-confidence, convincing us that alone we can do nothing.

This granite, which seems so unyielding and repellant, is really sensitively responsive to each fearful heart throb and plea for help. It guides our fingers and toes to exactly those places where we can gain the reassurance that we need. When fear is at its worst, then

97

God is closest, if we abandon ourselves to him in trust. The very immutability of the rock assures us that he is here, saying, "Fear not. It is I."

This does not prevent disordered imagination from experiencing this same rock as a monstrous impediment in our path, and the terrors and difficulties of clinging there as overwhelming. Our senses can find no comfort. Every foot and fingerhold seem to be gained on shifting, treacherous material. Disaster is imminent all the time, what is demanded is impossible. Imagination out of control turns the mind into a place of uncharted Himalayan peaks and precipices among which we are lost and in peril.

It is symptomatic of this state that, although reason assures us that our fears are overfanciful, it cannot quell the riot in our emotions. Only grace enables us to affirm our faith that exactly the opposite of what we imagine is the truth. The will can and does choose to trust God even while fear is indulging in an orgy of defeatist babbling. God has promised that he will not try us beyond our strength, and we have an obligation to believe him, as he has an obligation to help us. Humbly, we plead for this help, only too aware of what we are capable of doing if we do not receive it. We know we would opt out.

The cliff face can also be interpreted as the cross which at times seems so sheer and so stupendous that it stretches from heaven to hell. Those nailed upon it with Jesus in the dark night suffer a dizzying sense of being adrift in space, in the opposite of ecstatic levitation.

The things of the world and the senses have been left behind and are no longer even desired, but the perfection of pure faith, pure love and pure hope has not yet been attained, and even seems unattainable. Both what has been left behind and what is as yet beyond our reach, appear so far removed from us that they assume an air of unreality. The result is an impression of being strung up in midair, like a minute spider hanging from a thread far from any landfall, or like the alpinist who misses his foothold above the chasm, and dangles from his rope, swaying to and fro and unable to help himself.

Jesus said that when he was lifted up from the earth he would draw all things to himself. It is his magnetic force that makes us compulsively adhere to this cross in midair crucifixion, though terrified. Christ, in the famous Salvador Dali painting, has no nails in his hands and feet to keep his body upon his cross that hangs, itself without any visible support, high above a peaceful landscape, like a bird in flight. We are there with and in him, but nailed by our own dogged wills and sustained by grace. His divine will is powerful enough to keep him there without nails.

"With Christ I hang upon the cross"—and by means of this voluntary hanging "the world is crucified to me, and I to the world" (Gal 6:14). There are times in the spiritual life when this midair suspension in God's will is peaceful and consoling. In the passive purgations of the spirit it is crucifying and desolating.

On the tops of high mountains the air is pure but rare, and often there is not enough oxygen to breathe properly. So too, high up on this cliff face of a cross, we seem often to be gasping for air. There is a peculiar sense of being stifled and suffocated, which Jesus himself experienced physically because of the weight of his body bearing down on his internal organs, especially the heart and lungs, as he hung by the hands.

Our suffocation originates in our lack of sense experience of God in our dark, arid contemplation. He is very near, but he can be grasped only in the insensibility of bare faith. His love is pressing in upon the soul, but the soul has not yet developed the spiritual equipment to receive him fully in the form in which he is presenting himself—pure Spirit—and so feels smothered.

We are as yet so weak that we cannot absorb his reality. His inflowing presence makes us gasp and recoil, fearing to be crushed. Only the saints can live tranquilly in such close proximity to God, for they have lost themselves in him.

At this time we are enduring the spiritual equivalent of physical withdrawal symptoms from alcohol or drug addiction. We have been addicted to the things of sense, to the "affection of love" with all its ardors and attachments, to consolations and to the satisfaction of our spiritual appetites. God visited us with the sweet certainty of his presence. We were borne aloft on eagle's wings of grace. We experienced ourselves as chosen, safe, enfolded, comforted, at peace and secure in God and his will.

In reality all this was still more or less on the surface of the spiritual life; now we are being called to renounce it in favor of a much more radical abandonment to divine providence, a jump, blindfolded, into the inner abyss, a much deeper immersion in the Spirit, a rending open of locked doors, a prying apart of the will to receive the flooding in of the divine will, a departure from all that is understood into the incomprehensible depths of contemplation and the night of faith before the dawn.

God has called us by name and commanded, "Now you must give up all your addictions and cultivate only the addiction to me."

The experience of being suspended in space arises from the consent of our wills to God's command and his subsequent action. This is now at work in our inner abyss to detach us from the known and attach us only to the Trinity and its hidden life within us. Because this attachment is proceeding in a way that offers no emotional reassurances, but on the contrary the anguish of loss from our renunciations, and the craving for proofs of God's presence and love, we lack any assurance that we have attained it.

Having been cut off from the familiar, known and cherished, we have not yet been absorbed into the realm of the unfamiliar, unknown and feared. We hang in midair, crucified upon our poverty.

"The soul is now becoming alien and remote from common sense and knowledge of things, in order that, being annihilated in this respect, it may be informed with the divine—which belongs rather to the next life than to this" (D.N. II,IX,5).

A sense of estrangement is inevitable, for as human beings we are not geared to encounter and absorb what belongs to the next life rather than to this. We have lost what we had, but have not yet received the fulfillment of God's promise that those who give up everything for him will receive a hundredfold in recompense.

The crucifying sense of deprivation can cause intense suffering, for we cannot find comfort and ease anywhere or in anyone, and there is nothing to cling to for reassurance in the customary ways. Our grief becomes so great that we "imagine (we) are lost and (our) blessings have gone for ever. . . . At times this roaring and this affliction of the soul grow to such an extent that they overwhelm and penetrate it completely, filling it with spiritual pain and anguish in all its deep affections and energies, to an extent surpassing all possibility of exaggeration" (D.N. II,IX,7).

Such intense spasms of deprivation and suffering produce spiritual and emotional vertigo. We feel as if caught up in a whirlpool of unmeaning.

A whirlpool has a giddying fascination. It sucks its victims to destruction in some unknown, frightful depths. Once caught in its inexorable revolutions, there is no escape. Psychological and mental whirlpools are an apt symbol for certain forms of interior suffering where obsessive thoughts and feelings whirl ever faster and faster in a tightening coil.

There is a painting depicting the interior state of Jesus in Gethsemane that illustrates such dread. In a vortex like a whirlpool spinning to infinite depths are caught the symbols of his passion—cup of agony, thorns, nails, whips, jeering faces; and also those of humanity's passion—grief-eroded faces, torture instruments, soldiers, a burning city, a hangman's noose, a screaming child.

There are times when our inward being seems to writhe like a worm fast on a hook. The psalmist, referring to Jesus, said, "I am a worm, and no man." Jesus writhed in the mental and emotional torture of Gethsemane, lying on the ground and sweating blood. He writhed on the hook of the cross in his death agony, and with that hook he fished for, and caught, humanity. Lifted up on it, he drew all of us to himself by means of it. In the passive purgations we are writhing on that hook with him.

"In his will is our peace." The will of the Savior is that we should help him in his work, becoming suffering servants with him. To the degree that we accept and generously live out this vocation, we shall find peace. However, peace exists at different levels and in various ways within us, for we are wounded in our human nature in ways that Jesus never was. We are caught not only on the hook of the cross but trapped within the first syndrome.

Some kind of peace may be restored to the wounded psyche by bringing up to the surface powerful repressed elements and integrating them into the conscious personality in a process of recognition, acceptance and constructive use, as indicated in previous chapters. This involves a kind of purgation of the emotions and takes place on the psychological level. Such peace is not permanent, for human nature is in a state of chaos. We are victims of passions and drives that God intended to be under the control of will and reason. Right order has to be restored in our inner being on the spiritual level for peace to be genuine and effective. This order is essentially a work of grace where the human will becomes entirely subject in joyful submission to the divine will.

An absolutely necessary part of this work is learning to unite mental and emotional agonies with Christ's in his passion, thus making them positive and giving them a cosmic meaning and purpose.

The process of the divine reconstruction of personality so that it escapes from the confinement of the first syndrome (sin—suffering—evil) into the second (love—suffering—prayer) and finally into the third (love—joy—fulfillment) is initiated by baptism, but comes to fruition only when we are spiritually mature enough to submit to the passive purgations in our depths.

In Gethsemane, more than anywhere else in his passion, Jesus contained and experienced with and for us our mental and emotional torments. By becoming sin for us, and taking all our sins upon himself in his total innocence, he inevitably let himself become immersed in our sufferings, of which our psychological and emotional torments form a major part.

As this participation evinced itself in physical symptoms of acute distress, he must have felt himself being sucked into an infinite, eternal whirlpool of damnation centered in hell itself, for that was where we would all have found ourselves had he not taken away the sin of the whole world. The sensation must have recurred on Golgotha, especially in the cry of dereliction. Being like us in all things except sin, he must have endured mental and emotional as well as physical torment during his passion. He was tempted like us, though he never succumbed, so he must have been tempted to the ultimate sin of despair and final revolt against his Father's will.

Though we cannot plumb the mystery of the Savior's inner being, it is reasonable to suppose, since he was entirely human as well as entirely divine, that the above is true.

Returning to the whirlpool experience, we may say it is the gravitational force of innate sinfulness trying to suck us away from adherence to God's will. It draws us down into a primordial *angst*, into severance, loneliness and a panic search for meaning. We scrabble madly for foot or fingerhold where there is nothing but liquid insubstantiality. We cannot breathe. We feel vertigo and nausea. We endure the awful sensation of drowning in a filth that is our own and the race's sin, the first syndrome in its deepest and most concentrated essence.

We have an irrational, penetrating sense of being doom-laden and cursed. We know the anguish of unmeaning and the dread of what is yet to come. Having been made victims with the divine Victim, our minds threaten to overbalance into madness.

Our remedy lies in the practice of a faith certain that all such agonies, whatever their origin and level, can be rendered creative and redemptive, though not necessarily cured, by being deliberately made part of the interior sufferings of Jesus during his passion. This can entail heroic acts of faith made in the *Prayer of the Adamant Will*, during which we consciously merge our whirlpool with his cosmic one.

After such a degree of abandonment to God's action in us, it is impossible that his strange, consoling, nebulous yet rocklike peace should not be present in our depths, and that we should not be given the certainty that it is there. Those who suffer with Christ are privileged to be comforted, healed, revived and strengthened with Christ. God, beholding the Suffering Servant in them, pours out his mercy, pity and love just as he sent an angel into Gethsemane. The power to endure increases as grace increases. The penetrating *angst* is transmuted into creative, redemptive suffering. A readiness, even hunger, to stay with Christ in his passion for as long as God wills it grows in us.

The fact that we have let our sufferings of fear and grief drop into the whirlpool of Christ's anguish means that we will certainly become victors. Probably we will never feel we are, but this itself is a grace, for the more we experience ourselves as defeated failures, the more desperately we will plead for the grace to stop being sucked under, and the more we will seek and find our only refuge in Jesus.

"Take me, Lord, battered and half drowned as I am, and use me. I belong to you for your redemptive work through your church, the sacrament of salvation for the whole world." This is now our prayer.

The barriers of dread against God's awe-full inflowing have been demolished. We have let him and his grace come into our loneliest, most tormented, darkest places. Jesus walks upon the whirling waters, calming them. Peace rises up from those graced depths and we know we are saved and will be used to save others.

We experience one of those "enkindlings of love" of which John writes. Grace respites from the sufferings of the spiritual purgations, occur when we become submissive and open enough to receive the divine contemplation and love in the full force with which it is offering itself. The withdrawal symptoms cease, at least for a time, as we experience "a certain touch of the Divinity (which) is already the beginning of the perfection of the union of love for which (the soul) hopes" (*D.N.* II,XII,6).

Letter to a Bishop

Do you know how much you eased me
that dark winter afternoon last year
when I sat before you, fearful and tormented,
asking, "Do you think I'm mad?"
                              "Far from it!"

Today I write to tell you
those three firm words have stayed with me—
staunch staffs of faith to lean on when that snake
squirms round about me till he infiltrates
his Lord's domain.
He's been there all this week and will not be dislodged.

You once wrote that what I told you of myself
brought St. Teresa and her trials to your mind.
Today I want to tell you that your words "Far from it!"
were like the holy water she threw to dare
those devils torturing her to do their worst
for her Lord was with her in the night.

I had for years not opened to reread
that soaring eagle of a woman's breathless script—
her witness, among other things, of Satan's meddling
in her God-inebriated soul.
                         Today she spoke to me
as to a little sister: "I know just how it is for you
because that's how it was with me."

The devil's torture, she recorded, was intolerable,
    in fact, "like hell."

Her mind was darkened, incoherent and confused,
absurdities and turmoil splintering it. Peevishness

and even stupefaction, fogs and dizziness, illusion
    and dull idiocy
crammed that clear canyon of delight within her soul
where she had swooped with God in love-play's bliss.

She felt "a raving lunatic," directionless and dazed,
her life a maze of wandering round in circles, lost.
She pleaded with her Lord to "bind that lunatic"
and free this crazed, fragmented woman that she was
from evil bondage to an inner hell
and the "bad company" her soul was forced to keep.

Fray Peter, sane and saintly, came as a result,
told her prosaically, "Don't let it trouble you."
Brief and to the point for once, she notes
that she was "greatly comforted."

In my small, mean, ungainly way
I flipflop on this soaring eagle's trajectory,
to meet her face to face here in her chronicle.
Some minor incubus, intent on grounding me,
arrives spasmodically to carry out experimental work
and find how much my sanity can bear of calculated torture
before I too go babbling into lunacy
and rave until I suffocate in dread.

It was his machinations that last year
impelled my lurching spirit to your room.
Today, immersed in cyclical recurrence of my plight
and reading of Teresa and Fray Peter, I recall
my question and your answer.
                                        I am comforted.
I thank you. May God bless you. Barbara.

12 Enkindling and Respites

GOD'S TOUCH UPON the deepest inwardness of the self in the passive purgations brings joy as well as pain. The sufferings and privations of the passive purgations are interspersed with periods of consolation, peace and relief. During these the divine penetration is felt as a tender cherishing to which we cannot help but respond with a surge of reciprocal love.

God is wooing us in preparation for the final spiritual consummation. We experience that which, in his extended analogy of the log of wood, St. John calls "enkindling." During this enkindling, the "secret, peaceful and loving inflowing of God" (*D.N.* I,X,6) that is contemplation comes to us as blessing.

Suffering purges, but so does love. Since we are in love with Love himself, we are afflicted when it seems to us that he is spurning us. When he grants us a blissful foretaste of what is to come, we respond like those "deeply and passionately in love" (*D.N.* II,XI,1) who are being wooed by the beloved.

While the period of enkindling lasts, we do not recoil in fear from God's invasion but consent wholly and in delight. It is this total opening of ourselves that enables an act of full union to take place. Though it is transitory, it is of the same quality and intensity as the spiritual marriage. God gives himself; we receive. The love and longing are reciprocal.

Unified inwardly, we are unable to concentrate on, long for, immerse ourselves in, anything or anyone but him. There is right order within us. None of our emotional needs or obsessions have power to distract us from him and this gift of union while it is in progress. The once warring self-parts are either quiescent or else caught up in the surge toward the Beloved. "God alone! I want only God!" is our heart's cry. All our needs and desires are met because now our will is centered fully upon him and at rest in his will.

This is not the slaughter of the faculties, but their fulfillment in the Uncreated that can never pass away or betray. The will is totally re-collected from the interior dispersal and chaos that is our legacy from the first syndrome. The result is inner harmony, a diapason of praise of the Trinity with no jarring chords from unregenerate self-will and self-love to mar it.

This is the inclusive love spoken of in the first and great commandment, the totality of self-giving, the sanctification and even deification of all the faculties in the one supreme act of loving God perfectly and for himself. Recollection and enkindling depend upon one another until the will is gathered together and made whole in God's will. Perfection consists in this complete union of wills, and the consummation of mutual love flows from it.

Enkindling leads not only to joy, but to further suffering, for at this stage the heart is not permanently and completely cleansed. It is inflamed with painful longing both to receive and to give more and more love. At the same time the Spirit is causing awareness of dark patches and places in our depths that await rebirth. These now yearn to receive the infusion of grace and Presence also. The consequent suffering of deprivation and unworthiness blot out the awareness of enkindling elsewhere.

The heart's grief is magnified "by the spiritual darkness wherein it finds itself, which afflicts it with its doubts and misgivings; and then by the love of God, which enkindles and stimulates it, and, with its loving wound, causes it a wondrous fear" (D.N. II,XI,6). We see here how the four passions of joy, hope, fear and grief are at last all involved with and directed toward God.

The soul feels cramped because it longs to expand fully in God, but its own unresolved dark patches are preventing this expansion until the passive purgations have reached and cleansed them. The "affection of love" that at an earlier stage too often fastened itself compulsively and obsessively upon the created has now been transmuted into "spiritual affection," or longing, targeted upon the Creator himself. This spiritual affection is steadfast in its watching, waiting and hoping for the fullness of the divine invasion and upwelling.

John explains why and how we suffer when "this dark night of loving fire, as it purges in the darkness, so also in the darkness enkindles the soul" (D.N. II,XII,1). He juxtaposes fire, light and love with darkness, suffering, purging and deprivation, stressing how our whole experience of purgatory is a work of love. Wisdom is infusing into us the same contemplation as the angels enjoy in their vision of the Trinity in heaven. Pure spirits know as they are known. The passive purgations are enabling us to attain a similar state.

"God never grants mystical wisdom without love, since love itself infuses it . . . jointly, to each one according to his capacity and need" (*D.N.* II,XII,2).

In the hierarchy of created beings, humans are "the lowest of all those to whom this loving contemplation flows down continually from God." Because of our limited capacity, and our not being pure spirit, we receive God's ray of contemplation, or divine wisdom, only "in a very limited way and with great pain," for it is not natural for us to love and know in this way (*D.N.* II,XII,3).

It is as if we gazed at the sun with unprotected eyes and were blinded even while the glory of the sun was enkindling in us a love which in the end, if we let it, will spiritualize, refine and purge us. Then only will we be able to operate in the supernatural, angelic mode of perceiving that is a pure gift from God.

The enkindlings occur after the initial sufferings described in the earlier chapter on the log of wood, and after the understanding and the will have received many substantial touches from God, these touches being an experience of union, though it is not yet permanent. Enkindling is "a certain touch of the Divinity and is already the beginning of the perfection of the union of love for which (the soul) hopes" (*D.N.* II,XII,6).

This ebb and flow of the spirit, passively infusing life and love into us, is something we must not try either to control or induce. God acts at times like a playful human lover who teases, incites, flirts, advances and then withdraws, leading on the beloved only to deny final consummation. At times he visits and enkindles the understanding, yet leaves the will arid and in pain from longing for him. At other times he floods the will with an ecstasy of love, but leaves the understanding blinded by an intensity of contemplation that registers on it only as afflictive darkness.

He wounds the heart, but at the same time causes it to expand and flame with love so that it can scarcely bear the intensity and even longs to die. This, of course, helps to cleanse it of what is preventing the consummation of love. By capturing the will he causes it to love with his own divine love for "this heat of love strikes the substance of the soul, and thus moves the affections passively" (*D.N.* II,XIII,3). This happens with the will's consent, for it is not being forced to love, but having its deepest longing to be able to love satisfied as it opens itself to the inflowing.

Both the thirst for and the enkindling of love at this stage of the soul's progress toward full union belong to the spirit rather than sense or emotions. These are not obliterated, but now originate in the heart's spiritual hunger for the Spirit. Its realization and experience of its own lack are much stronger and deeper than anything felt in the night of sense, so that the enkindling, when it happens, far surpasses any earlier, more surface sweetnesses and consolations.

Various forms or aspects of spiritual love goad the heart toward reckless abandonment to God's action and entry. It is given a reverent love of the wonderful qualities and perfections of the Trinity, so that by comparison everything created has only reflected luster. The seat of this love is in the understanding and intelligence, yet it is not something intellectually perceived but rather infused and grasped intuitively all in an instant.

The will is granted the grace of inebriation of love. This induces a boldness in yearning for even fiercer enkindlings.

As the heart is drawn deeper into union, these gifts of love alternately cause delight and suffering. The heart is torn between affliction that it is unworthy and unready to receive God, and that he will therefore never fulfill its longings and grant it pure joy, and exultation that he is using it as a repository for his love, and that it can suffer for him and so share in the Savior's redemptive work. At times the grace of inebriation is so overwhelming that its possessor acts strangely as if actually drunk. We are reminded of the apostles under the influence of the Spirit, of whom observers laughingly said, "They have been drinking too much new wine" (Acts 2:13).

The human lover is so totally captivated by the Beloved that she is reckless in her attempts to reach him, receive him, do as he wishes. The force and determination imbuing action can be frightening in their boldness and disregard of possible results such as condemnation by others or hurt to oneself. The vehemence of love is so great that it perseveres against impossible odds.

Such intensity of love has driven the saints to tackle and accomplish seemingly foolhardy and incredible feats in God's service, sacrificing themselves in the process, even to being martyred. His infinite, compassionate love in caring for the afflicted, unloved and unwanted has possessed others wholly, as it has Mother Teresa of Calcutta in our times.

This same love causes them brokenheartedly to condemn themselves as the worst of sinners and unworthy of God's attentions, for union with his Perfection has revealed to them in pitiless clarity their own imperfections.

It is important to remember when we ourselves are overwhelmed by the graced awareness of our own sinfulness that "the darkness and the other evils of which the soul is conscious when this Divine light strikes it, are not darkness or evils caused by this light, but pertain to the soul itself, and the light illumines it so that it may see them" (*D.N.* II,XIII,10). It is God's mercy that shows us how we really are in relation to his perfect purity and sinlessness. His purpose is to make us humble enough to be his vessels of election.

The enkindlings of love and light, whether they induce delight in union or shame at our own unworthiness, occur once we have been purified enough to be able to bear them. The work of passive purification is accomplished through them, whichever effect they have, and because of them every aspect of our inner being is "changed and converted divinely, according to God. And thus this soul will now be a soul of heaven, heavenly, and more divine than human" (*D.N.* II,XIII,11).

This is the scriptural state of the kingdom of heaven within. It is what Paul writes about when he says, "Life to me, of course, is Christ" (Phil 1:21); "You have died, and now the life you have is hidden with Christ in God" (Col 3:3); "The Spirit of God has made his home in you" (Rom 8:9); "I am become Christ!"

However, the fullness of this state is not attained permanently until the passive purgations are completed. Until then the enkindlings are intermittent tastes of it that encourage and strengthen us to submit to even deeper and more painful inflowings of God into the abyss of our inner selves.

Whether they come or not, and to what degree of intensity, depends upon two factors—the Spirit's judgment as to whether this is the right time, and our own readiness and openness.

They may not come at all in any way of which we are conscious. Therese, for example, though a saint, seems never to have experienced them, or only once or twice in a transitory way. In this respect, it is important to remember that she had offered herself as a victim of divine love. Perhaps that same Love deprived her of the grace of consoling awareness of his presence, so the grace could be applied to some sinner lost in his sin, in order to convert him. Yet it is undoubtedly true that she was blessed with the highest state of union with the Trinity.

Such matters must remain mysteries to us.

To those in the night of the spirit, the enkindlings will normally come in one form or another, and more or less at spaced intervals. They will vary in intensity and length from a momentary penetration, a mere flick of the Presence, as it were, that yet pierces us with awareness and even with an almost unbearable intensity of love, to day-long celebrations of festival and hosanna that change the way we perceive ourselves, others and reality itself.

Certain dispositions are necessary before such visitations can and will occur, though God, of course, does not observe any rules. Some of the main ones are:

1) An Advanced Degree of Detachment

Growing in detachment through the shedding of attachments goes on till death, no matter how spiritually mature a person may be. Attachments begin with the grosser, material ones. Genuine conversion initiates the struggle against these. Then come the attachments to various consolations of the early stages of the spiritual life, to our own wills in the service of God, to certain forms of prayer, to people, places, things, to psychological and emotional satisfactions and aberrations, to apparently harmless and obviously harmful habits, desires and drives.

The active and passive nights of sense attack these.

Then there are the more spiritual and deeply rooted attachments, often very subtle and hard to discern, and all the more dangerous for that. All of these are forms of clinging to our own will and indulging self-love and self-interest. The active night of the spirit and finally the passive purgations are aimed at their elimination.

We do not easily give them up, and until inner space has been made for him by their casting out, God does not ordinarily come into our hearts with his spiritual enkindlings and most penetrating graces. Space for him is made by our becoming detached from even our holiest attachments, and by constant vigilance against fostering new ones.

"You must know that the forces of self-love which was born along with us are such that we have no sooner detached it from a good than it attaches itself to another with the same ardour; and that without changing its unfortunate character, it for the most part merely changes its object, transforming its natural affections, transporting them from temporal goods to spiritual ones, that we usually love in relation to ourselves more than to God. Now this new attachment is the more harmful in that, since it appears holy and praiseworthy, the heart gives itself up to it without a struggle, without thought and even with an ardour and zeal with which we feel very satisfied, because we regard it as true zeal for our salvation and perfection. Yet this deep and ardent zeal often comes merely from the same background of attachment to holy things that we see in worldly people for profane things" (Caussade, *On Prayer*, p. 244).

The attachment-detachment cycle goes on unendingly throughout the spiritual life. The heart compulsively reaches out in an effort to satisfy its longings with lesser goods rather than make the painful renunciation of them in favor of the only everlasting, incorruptible, absolute Good.

The more spiritual an attachment the more harmful it can be, for the heart embraces it gratefully and joyfully, deluded into the conviction it is a gift from God. It may be—but not for us to attach our hearts to. The proof of our good faith is whether we gladly relinquish whatever or whoever it is when God, usually working through the circumstances of our lives, deprives us of it.

2) *Purity of Intention*

If we have this we shall be able to make such a relinquishment gladly with the will, even if suffering emotionally.

Purity of intention means to love and to live for the honor and glory of God rather than to feed our own self-love, and because this attachment is his will rather than because our own self-will dictates it.

Easy to say, extremely difficult to do, for no matter how honest we try to be with ourselves, the drive to self-deceit is innate. The I AM, the primeval Eve, have no intention of being put down. They want what they want, so they have evolved all manner of subtle, devious ways of confusing issues, encouraging rationalizations, and leading us down side tracks instead of straight up the *nada* path, which is very much a way of total detachment and purity of intention.

If we have these virtues, we are malleable in God's hands. We change direction readily and immediately, if he wills it. We renounce today the graces and blessings he gave us yesterday, if he requires it. We want only what he wants, when he wants it and in the way he wants.

Self-interest and disinterestedness must have been long at war within us before we attain that purity of intention that can say to the Beloved, "I long for you from my deepest depths. I yearn for your visitation. Nevertheless, not my will, but yours be done. Come when you are ready, because only your wisdom knows when I am ready. In the meantime I submit, wait and fast."

When he sees we desire his enkindling and his graces and gifts primarily because they will glorify and honor him, and very much secondarily for the joy, fulfillment and holiness they bring us, then he will come.

3) *Holy Indifference*

This quality is not the same as apathy. As lovers of Christ we have a life of service to live within the community, and we cannot be indifferent to the presence of good and evil there, in other people, and in ourselves. We are called to positive action that will foster the good and eliminate evil.

Holy indifference is concerned with the results of our actions. We do our best, but the results are in God's hands. If we have a pure intention of acting out of love for him and neighbor, then we also have holy indifference regarding the outcome. We trust divine providence to bring about the results it knows are best for these circumstances and these people.

If this means the defeat of all our plans and the destruction of our good works, we accept this as God's will, mysterious and crucifying though it is, reminding ourselves that Jesus saved the world through what appeared at the time to be total defeat.

"It is the disinterestedness of perfect love, which delivers us from the slavery of self-love, from its unquiet urgings, from its grievous troubles, from its endless fears about everything concerning our greatest interests, the salvation of the soul, advancement, progress, eternal beatitude, for if we seek thenceforth entirely or chiefly the holy will of God, we nobly abandon all the success of our quest to him" (Caussade, p. 249).

After our painful struggles with our self-love and self-will have resulted in a degree of holy indifference, there will be space in us for the Trinity to come and dwell within. Enkindling will occur, and the impact of the spiritual fulfillment will itself infuse an even deeper holy indifference. Paradoxically, even while we delight in the Presence and drink deep of the living waters, we shall grow in detachment, so that we shall be able to let God go and not grieve and cling when the enkindling fades away. We now know with complete conviction that the possession of God and union with him consist not in any "experiences," however sublime, but in the perfect merging of our will with his.

4) *Poverty of Spirit*

The above qualities, together with a high degree of self-abandonment to divine providence, are what make up poverty of spirit.

The perfectly poor in spirit dwell as servants in the peace of their own humility, waiting upon God and his will, wanting nothing for themselves except what he wants for them, cleansed of all impetuosity, self-aggrandizement, over-zealousness, and urge to choose what they want instead of letting the Spirit choose for them.

They remain in peace where God places them, occupied with carrying out his signified will and their obvious duties, with praising and loving him in their hearts, content with the present (as long as it neither contains nor leads to sin), detached from the past, unconcerned and unpreoccupied with the future. Having let him strip them of every attachment, material, temporal and spiritual, they leave it to him to clothe their nakedness with the garments of his choice, when and how he sees fit.

Thus they are both free and at peace, and ready for the final enkindling that is transforming union, when they will be fully clothed in Christ.

Before such a state of heroic abandonment is reached, however, further and more excruciating purgations must occur.

The enkindlings have encouraged and strengthened us spiritually to bear these. If we keep ourselves open to God, he will lead us
into the final stage, which is best likened to the dying and entombment of Jesus, after which came his resurrection. He has summoned
us to participate fully in this whole death-rebirth cycle. We must be
crucified and die with him if we are to rise with him to the new life
of transforming union.

In Praise of God's Two Hands

Your one hand cups me in your sheltering palm—
this insignificant insect that is I
lately emerged from metamorphosis, now quivering
in expectation.
           I agitate
my gauzy wings, alert for currents of warm air
to lift me high into the sun-drenched spaces.
I wait, antennae tremulous,
my tiny, vulnerable form
readied for flight.

Instantaneous, out of this cloudless sky,
eclipse falls.
           Upon your concave palm
your other hand bears down. The two
clamp shut as tight as oyster shells.
I, trapped within, discover night.

Stifled, oppressed, I flutter in bewilderment and fear.
Then crouch inert in darkness, grieving for the sun,
the radiance of open skies, inviting me
to be myself and fly.
                         I cannot move. I feel
as if a mighty weight, annihilation's tool,
is crushing me, expelling life.

Here is no time. I die, but yet remain aware
I do not die. I live bereft of life.

Then, instant as your hand swept down,
it lifts and disappears.
    Ah, light! It cascades merrily
to fill the death-cell space with joy.
It warms my sun-starved, frozen form.

You cry, exulting, to me, "The time has come to fly,
you tiny aspect of my endless love!"
In one grand gesture then, you toss me upwards
so I find my wings and what you made me for.
Intoxicated by such vastnesses of height and space
I dart and swoop
in ecstasies of flight.

13 Submit—Wait—Fast

In the passive purgations of the spirit, we are one with Jesus in his passion, co-workers with him in his body, the universal sacrament of salvation. He has gone before us, entering into and embracing all our darknesses, and so making it possible for us to do the same. Always his strength is being made perfect in our weakness if only we will let him in to work upon that weakness.

We have nothing to lose but the chains that bind our hearts so we are unable to will unreservedly what God wills, no matter how hard we try. Only through the night of the spirit can we reach freedom, and so a last rest, without a quiver of revulsion, in his will at every level, and regarding all aspects of our life, inner and outer.

In Gethsemane and throughout his passion and in his dying, Jesus shows us how to endure these purgations in a spirit of total abandonment. Though he had no need of purgations himself, the way in which he met his sufferings gives us a perfect example of how to meet ours.

His two key prayers were, "Nevertheless, not my will, but yours be done," and, "Into your hands I commit my spirit."

From the moment of his Gethsemane prayer of acceptance till his death on the cross, he was in a state of total passivity and abandonment. He made no effort either to justify himself or escape, and even rebuked the disciples for being prepared to defend him.

To Pilate he said, "You would have no power over me, were it not given you on high," indicating that he knew all those involved in the events of his passion were merely instruments of God doing what had to be done so he could fulfill his destiny.

His whole being answered one continuous "Amen" to everything. There was no quiver of evasion or revolt anywhere in him. "I and the Father are one," he had said. Now he demonstrated this in his perfect obedience to and acceptance of his fate and the working out of the divine will, of which he himself as the second person of the Trinity was an inseparable element.

He commanded us to take up our cross daily and follow him. This means practicing the same perfect obedience and abandonment throughout the severest sufferings of our life. In purgatory after death all must be in this state. They have no alternative, no power of choice. But in purgatory in this life, we do have the choice of assenting to or repudiating God's will, and so we can add to his glory and honor and our own holiness by letting the Trinity invade us ever more deeply to use us ever more accurately and fully.

Throughout his writings, and particularly in the *Ascent* and *Dark Night*, John of the Cross stresses the absolute need for the human will to conform perfectly to God's if transforming union is to be attained. "The state of this divine union consists in the soul's total transformation, according to the will, in the will of God, so that there may be naught in the soul that is contrary to the will of God, but that, in all and through all, its movement may be that of the will of God alone" (*Ascent* I,XI,2).

We do not need simply to obey God's will, but to do so out of love. His will is the means he uses to bring us all the love and goodness of his perfectly loving and good divine nature. In whatever form it presents itself, it is to be reverenced and embraced with an active love going far beyond lukewarm resignation. To love his will is to love God.

Those enduring the passive purgations of the spirit have long ago reached this state of renunciation of their own will in favor of God's, and out of love for him. But they are not yet perfect in the virtue of abandonment to divine providence.

There are still movements, largely involuntary, of revulsion and rebellion. Struggles are still necessary before acceptance is immediate and wholehearted. There is still a tendency to bargain with God, to try to wheedle him out of requiring a particular self-denial of us in favor of another suggested by us to him.

Above all, we still have hidden attachments and desires that prevent us from complete, instant obedience and abandonment.

"For it comes to the same thing whether a bird be held by a slender cord or by a stout one. . . . Because (certain souls) have not the resolution to break with some whim or attachment or affection . . . they never make progress or reach perfection, though they would need to do no more than make one good flight, and thus snap that cord of desire right off, or to rid themselves of that sucking-fish of desire which clings to them" (*Ascent* I,XI,4).

Often we ourselves are oblivious of these attachments and desires that our wills cling to in spite of wanting not to cling to anything. Once our conscious will genuinely longs and strives to be completely one with his will, God takes pity on us and does for us what we cannot do for ourselves—he himself breaks the cord holding the bird from flight, while we passively submit, though sometimes we complain and chide him. It may be a long time before we can accept and admit that this was the best thing that could have happened to us.

Human nature remains human nature, even in the night of the spirit. However submission, though we cannot make it immediate, is an essential part of abandonment.

Often we feel unable to submit to what God lets happen to us because we cannot understand why and how. But if we could understand, there would be no need of faith and abandonment, and these are two of the virtues that must reach the heroic level before we can enter full love-union with the Trinity.

The how and the why of the workings of divine providence are and always will be beyond our understanding. That the benign process of love centering itself in creation gone awry goes on without interruption, we can believe. We can extend that faith to seeing the whole of history as well as each second of our own life being under the same all-loving influence and guidance. But to reach the stage where the itch to know why and how has vanished requires a much greater degree of trust.

> How can God let this happen to children?
> Why doesn't he provide a cure for cancer?
> Why should this happen to me?
> Why didn't he stop it? He's omnipotent, isn't he?
> How can this possibly be his will?
> How can he be at work through such an absurd tragedy?
> Why doesn't he prevent wars?
> How can I tell that this is really his will?
> Why should I accept the defeat of all my plans?

When Peter protested at having his feet washed, Jesus said, "At the moment you do not know what I am doing, but later you will understand" (Jn 13:7).

The stronger the faith, the less need for the intellect to fiddle with the how and the why, and the deeper the patient submission evinced towards God's action. To submit means to give up our rights (as we see them) voluntarily to him, as Jesus in Gethsemane chose to give up his rights as Son of God and submit to his destiny as representative man, letting events take their inexorable course, certain that they were expressing the Father's will, which of course was also his own.

His will was at rest in God's because it desired nothing and no one but the Father. He had inner peace right down to those depths where desires originate. When he said, "My peace I give you, but not as the world gives peace," he was offering us this absolute repose in God, attainable if we would join him in his perfect submission, and not attainable by the fulfillment of any earthly, personal desires.

St. Francis de Sales' rule for himself was, "Desire nothing. Ask nothing. Refuse nothing." This was exemplified perfectly by Jesus in his passion once he had accepted the cup in Gethsemane. Our pattern is similar as we endure the passive purgations in our depths where our self-will and self-love are making their final stand.

"The divine action sees in the Word the idea in accordance with which you have to be formed; this idea is your exemplar" (Caussade, *Self-abandonment to Divine Providence*, p. 39).

God is busy forming the Son in us in all his completeness, though tailored to our individuality, and we cannot expect his passion and death will be omitted. How can we know what secret attractions, desires, attachments are binding us there in the hidden fastnesses of our hearts? We do not know, so we cannot ask to be delivered from them in any specific way of our own choice, but must leave the Spirit to work it out for us.

What we do know is that our "Father knows what [we] need before [we] ask him" (Mt 6:8), and that "when we cannot choose words in order to pray properly, the Spirit himself expresses our plea in a way that could never be put into words, and God who knows everything in our hearts knows perfectly well what he means, and that the pleas of the saints expressed by the Spirit are according to the mind of God" (Rom 8:26-27).

We are not yet saints, but that does not stop the Spirit from pleading for exactly what he knows we need, if only we submit to not knowing ourselves what it is and leave him to go about his intercessory business in his own way and time. The only prayer we ourselves are capable of is the dumb allegiance of the will.

This means that as well as submitting, we have to wait.

Jesus waited until his hour came, and he was shown when it had arrived. Events caught him up and he let himself be carried along by them much as a gull, hawk or eagle soars in the sky, using the air currents and thermals to glide in, effortlessly abandoned to the air with no need to flap its wings, yet in control of itself.

At any time, Jesus could have summoned legions of angels to his rescue, but he chose to remain in the surge of divine providence in action, letting himself be borne along, willing whatever it willed.

Having waited till God said, "Now," he was instrumental in his own destiny by paradoxically submitting to the divine intervention in human events.

To wait in patience is possible only for those who are free of attachments and desires, which means self-love and self-will. When Milton wrote in his sonnet on his own blindness, "They also serve who only stand and wait," he showed deep spiritual insight into the condition of those enduring the passive purgations. Of their very nature they require us to "stand and wait"—to stand fast whatever happens, and to wait however fiercely tempted to run away or take matters into our own hands.

There is a time for using our own initiative and acting, and a time for standing back and waiting to see what will happen instead of making it happen. Only the Spirit's gift of discernment can help us know what is demanded of us when.

To be able to wait upon God's will in peace is a great grace and brings even greater graces.

"By waiting and by calm you shall be saved, in quiet and in trust your strength lies. The Lord is waiting to show you favor; blessed are all who wait for him" (Breviary prayer).

God waits until we have learned the art of waiting upon him. Then, when at last we have stopped thrusting obstructions in the way of his divine providence, he is able to direct it in a flood upon us so that we are swept along by it, unprotesting, to what he knows is our destiny. If we have already defined our destiny for ourselves, we may be in for some rather unsettling surprises.

Waiting is the special work of those in the purgatorial state. They can have no idea how long their purification will last or what form it will take. All they can do is submit and wait for God's will to work itself out to its ordained outcome, using what is already present (or lacking) within them, and also the events, circumstances and necessary duties of their lives. God arranges what he wants in the way he wants if only we let him manipulate us as he wants.

The third requirement for heroic self-abandonment is to fast. "'But the time will come, the time for the bridegroom to be taken away from them; that will be the time when they will fast'" (Lk 5:35).

At the last supper Jesus told the disciples he must leave them. When they protested, he added that unless he left, the Spirit he was to give them would not come to them.

Earlier in our spiritual life, on a lower level of the *nada* path, we experienced the bridegroom's presence in and with us, and the bliss he brought with him. Now he leaves us in crucifying aridity, loneliness and desolation as he goes to his passion and death within us. His purpose is to make us ready to receive that ultimately penetrating action of the Spirit in our depths that will sanctify us, finally uniting us with the Trinity in spiritual marriage.

If he does not go to Calvary in and with us, this will not happen. Of course he does not really leave us. We know in faith that all Three continue to make their home in us as long as we ourselves do not drive them out by sinning. What he requires of us is that we should submit to fasting from the awareness and experiential tasting of that presence in order to be fitted for the even greater and more subtle, penetrating graces he wishes to bestow when his time (not ours, except in relation to his) arrives.

We perhaps thought we were ready. He knows we are not. We have to fast even from the longing and desire for him.

T.S. Eliot, writing of just this stage of the spiritual life in *East Coker* in his *Four Quartets*, and also paraphrasing John of the Cross, puts it this way:

I said to my soul, be still, and wait without hope

> For hope would be hope for the wrong thing;
>   wait without love
> For love would be love for the wrong thing;
>   there is yet faith
> But the faith and the love and the hope are all
>   in the waiting.

The spiritually dispossessed submit, wait and fast from hope and love. The bridegroom is busy on his cross and they must fast from the tenderness of his love. He is still and lifeless in the tomb, and fasting from light, joy and fulfillment, they must lie down with him and be obliterated, precisely so he may raise them up into the third syndrome when the right time comes.

John assures us, "Although this happy night brings darkness to the spirit, it does so only to give it light in everything; and, although it humbles it and makes it miserable, it does so only to exalt it and to raise it up; and, although it impoverishes it and empties it of all natural affection and attachment, it does so only that it may enable it to stretch forward, divinely, and thus to have fruition and experience in all things, both above and below, yet to preserve its unrestricted liberty of spirit in them all" (*D.N.* II,IX,1).

John warns, like a stern schoolmaster, that "one single affection remaining in the spirit, or one particular thing to which, actually or habitually, it clings" (*D.N.* II,IX,1) is enough to prevent us from entering the blessed and blissful spiritual state he has described. No wonder we must fast before such a festival. No wonder we have to be stripped naked of every attachment and desire, however seemingly unimportant, before we are clean and pure of heart enough to be clothed in that particular wedding garment of grace prepared especially and separately for each one of us.

This fasting means letting God take things and people away from us in a real and agonizing deprivation. He acts—and we suffer the act in as total an abandonment as we can muster.

Festival and Vigil

"It seems to the soul as if, before celebrating that festival,
    it has first been made to keep that vigil."
                                    —St. John of the Cross

How can such a festival be celebrated
without a fast and vigil coming first?

Bare floors and table, uncurtained windows
dark and blank against a starless night.
A hard bed lacking sheet and blanket,
cold water in tin basin on a makeshift stand,
long hours of kneeling on a pitiless board
before an unlit candle in a chilly room
stripped of all adornments.
Dry bread, a little salt and water,
and the uncompromising book
open at a paradoxical text.

Who can believe
immersed in poverty and pain
that festival will follow?
Vigil give place to rich fulfillment?
Hunger to feasting and delight?
Longing to embrace?
Cold to warmth?
Loss to love?

Keep vigil.
Fast.
Believe.
And hope.

14 Cleansing Human Relationships

THE PASSIVE PURGATIONS are very much to do with the purification of the emotions, with directing them to the right objects with the appropriate intensity, with severing them from attachments hindering God's total possession of the heart, with controlling the self-indulgence involved in their uninhibited expression, with giving them over entirely to the Spirit so they become the servants of her will to love.

In the active nights we have already done all we could, under our own power plus helping grace, to bring about the above adjustments. At a certain stage we reach an impasse. There is a sense of wonders having been accomplished, but this is coupled with a niggling intuition that much, much more needs to be done, only we are incapable of doing it, and anyway, it is not yet quite the right time.

God will have to do it for and in us while we wait.

Eventually he sends the Spirit to perform the sanctifying work of infusing divine love into us while we remain docile and receptive.

The passive purgations are a crucifixion of the Eve-Adam self, with all its tumultuous passions and urgent, disorderly needs and drives. Only after this comes our resurrection into the new Christ-self where Jesus will use our hearts and emotions for the expression of his own love.

This entails a transformation, a lifting up, as Christ himself was lifted up on the cross, a bursting forth into new life of the baptismal seed buried in the ground of our being. The result is an exalted life at a high level of spiritual evolution.

In this transformation all the natural faculties are supernaturalized by having the Spirit infused into them, and this includes the emotions, since they are such an important, vital part of our human equipment. They are not destroyed, but raised up and sanctified in Christ.

Paul's words about the resurrection of the dead have an application here. "The thing that is sown is perishable, but what is raised is imperishable; the thing that is sown is contemptible, but what is raised is glorious; the thing that is sown is weak, but what is raised is powerful; when it is sown it embodies the soul, when it is raised it embodies the spirit" (1 Cor 15:42-44).

God the Spirit, married to that matter from which our emotions originate, conceives and brings forth the Son in them. The Spirit overshadows us in our anguished struggle to get free from the tyranny of the Eve-Adam enslavement, takes these primordial elements tenderly into his infinite love and turns them into spiritual forces of extraordinary glory, power and energy.

We remain human, so the emotions are not destroyed but made capable of heavenly reactions instead of only earthly ones. They become ethereal, like the Bach *Art of the Fugue*, where before they had resembled a lush, fruity presentation by Mantovani and his orchestra of some popular love songs.

In heaven we shall remain human beings, but spiritualized, exalted humans, as Christ was when he appeared to the women and disciples between his resurrection and ascension. In this life and still on earth, God calls certain people to witness to this spiritualized but still human state of being. Before they can do so, they must endure a reorganization of the heart's powers.

"For one single affection remaining in the spirit, one particular thing to which, actually or habitually, it clings, suffices to hinder it from feeling or experiencing or communicating the delicacy and intimate sweetness of the spirit of love" (*D.N.* II,IX,1).

It is natural for us to want to choose our love objects, and to do so spontaneously and for our own satisfaction with a greater or lesser degree of altruism involved. The term love is applied to such a wide range of human relationships, emotional involvements and sexual attractions, that little consensus exists of what exactly is meant.

Since those who are in the passive purgations have long ago reached a certain level of unselfish service of others, with or without emotional involvement, and have spent years struggling to purify their intentions in their relationships with humans and God, for them love already means something positively altruistic.

But however great their efforts, and however sincere their belief that they are loving as Jesus wants them to, their love is still tainted with very deep-rooted elements of self-seeking aimed at fulfillment of hidden urges, needs and lacks in themselves.

These drive them, in spite of themselves, to use others in subtle ways, to bargain with God, to be deluded about the quality of their loving, to become deeply attached to and emotionally involved with their beloveds in a way that is distracting and hindering to their spiritual development.

Human relationships are of the utmost importance in the spiritual life because through them we normally learn about loving and being loved, gradually find out what the two great commandments are about, grow to emotional maturity and begin to understand the quality of God's love for us and how we can love him.

It is well known that a child with loving parents, whom she trusts and loves in return, grows into an adult able to love and trust others, and also God. A child unloved, unwanted, abused, starved of companionship and all the affectionate expressions of love grows into a socially and emotionally maladjusted adult who may be a psychopath, and who very likely will find it impossible to trust and love God or believe God loves her.

These are generalizations, but such patterns do exist often enough for us to be sure there is plenty of truth in them.

In a sense the unloved and unwanted have had their hearts crucified before ever they begin their journey to God, if they ever do begin. Yet these same crucified hearts may compel them to seek in God someone who will not betray or spurn them.

The loved and wanted, the blessed and fulfilled on the human level, on the other hand, may be handicapped in unexpected ways. Because they find, and have found, human love so satisfying, they may have little drive to seek divine love.

Whoever we are and whatever our circumstances, Jesus may choose any one of us at any stage of our life and command peremptorily, "Come. Follow me." If we answer the call and do not give up, one day we shall be summoned to a radical detachment from all our love objects. However much we have already given up for God, he will reveal to us how much we have yet to give, to what degree emotional involvment with cause, work, people, our own spiritual life "experiences," even our own concept of him is making us evade the spiritualization of the emotions and so cling to our own wills instead of relinquishing absolutely everything and everyone to the control of his will.

He produces in us a desire for this final purification to be done to and in us, and for the right reason—so that he will be honored and glorified through us far, far more than he can be in our present state of subtle, deep-rooted egoism.

Jesus said a house divided against itself would fall. Our inner house has had all its visible levels cleansed and put in order in an admirable fashion. But in the cellars, hidden too deeply to be seen or heard, are a few reprehensible creatures we never knew we were giving house room to. They have repetitive chants like "I won't serve. . . . I want my own way—and I'm going to get it. . . . I'm starved for love and no one's going to stop me from grabbing at it. . . . I want—I want—I want. . . . "

These chants seep up to the well-organized, controlled upper rooms, but on the way the words mysteriously change, losing their blunt realism.

They issue as insidious rationalizations; little, quiet, sedate dramas that have the desired result of our getting our own way; genteel manipulations of loved ones so they will bestow on us the kind of cherishing we need and want; assurances to ourselves that such a beautiful relationship must be in accordance with God's will and to his honor and glory; clever little plans to stop us being separated from our loved one; concepts of holiness that fit in with the ways we have devised of getting the emotional satisfaction we need; sublimation of gross cravings into more subtle, disguised and therefore dangerous ones; fixed ideas about what are acceptable, spiritualized ways of expressing holy tenderness, and so forth.

Self-deceit and unconscious delusion are at work here, hindering perfect purity of intention, holy indifference and poverty of spirit. There is no deliberate sin involved, but there is a general, involuntary lack of simplicity, originating in what the will cannot control because it cannot reach it and is probably oblivious of its existence.

All this is going to be thrown up to the surface. In the process, some relationships are going to be broken or damaged. There will be misunderstandings, bitterness, recriminations, disgust, fierce urges to wound as we are being wounded, exposure of our most sen-

sitive, shameful areas, tramplings all over them, humiliations beyond bearing, glaring revelations of the truth of what we've been
up to (all unknowingly), in short, the apparent collapse into ruins of
much of this orderly, clean, well-lit and respectable edifice we
called our spiritual life.

If we had not already advanced so far, the collapse would not
be so devastating. In actual fact, only the accidents of our personal
relationships have fallen into ruins. The substance, that includes
our sincerity, our decades of effort to fit ourselves to be a dwelling-
place for the Trinity, our helpless, faithful, yearning love for God
and his will, our certainty that we cannot live without his love and
grace—these, and much more, including what were the realities instead of the romanticisms, of our relationships with our beloveds—
all these remain.

They are still solidly evident, like the framework of a house after the walls and roofing have been stripped off. What is more, the
cellars have now been laid open, the rebellious creatures inhabiting
them exposed, and through that exposure reduced to manageable
proportions and made eligible for the direct action of grace.

Having been so severely chastened, we are now much humbler
than before. Because our sincerity and commitment were real, we
have been able to accept the truths that have been revealed to us,
and probably also to others. After an immense struggle with self-
love, we have let grace in to do its work. God's action can now happen in our depths.

Those depths are already praying, "Maranatha. Come, Lord Jesus." Spiritualization of the emotions has to be a product of grace, for it
entails imbuing the natural with the supernatural. All unknown to
ourselves, we were wanting and willing this to happen, for we really
did long to love God with all our being, though with one part of ourselves we went on compulsively playing our games of love.

We were ready to relinquish all the emotional satisfactions and
fulfillments that had entranced, captivated and involved us, only
we could not quite bring ourselves to make the decisive step. God
had to do it for us.

It is the difference between Mantovani and Bach. We were
willing to give up Mantovani, but could not make ourselves turn off
the stereo and throw away the tape or record. We have now done
this and so exchanged romanticism for reality.

Caussade teaches that after many heroic struggles against attachments and releases from them, "The most delicate, the most continual, that which is least recognized and dearest to the heart, still remains; it is what the mystics call the attachment to the proprietary use of the faculties" (Caussade, *On Prayer*, p.250).

We had already given up everything we could for and to God. We had done our best to merge our will totally with his, to love with his love, to deny our hearts anything that we thought was not part of his design for us.

But under all this, and in spite of our deep sincerity, we had clung to "the spirit of self-ownership"—the secret determination to let God do what he liked with us, as long as he did it in the manner we preferred or chose. We had our own convictions about the way to reach perfect love, and though we had operated submissively in the areas his will dictated for us, we followed our own notions of *how* we would do it.

We clung to our preconceived notions of how relationships should develop and mutual love be expressed. There was no excessive attachment. The imperfection was in the subtle way we directed things ourselves, taking initiatives and imposing patterns.

We had followed our own particular inclinations in our relationships, instead of leaving them open-ended for God, not us, to manipulate.

Caussade writes, "This is their exercise of the spirit of self-ownership, their real independence even, in their usage of the holiest of their powers, already consecrated to God in the *matter* of their actions, but not in the *manner* of their performance. Now God wants everything, as he deserves everything" (*On Prayer*, p. 250).

It is our choice whether or not we let in the Spirit to perform this last cleansing in the depths of our hearts, so God may indeed have everything we have to give him. It is easy to turn away our gaze from what is revealed to us, convince ourselves there is no deliberate sin involved, which is true, and go on as we are. We have been given understanding of what is the obstruction impeding the divine inflowing. Our part now is to will its removal.

If instead we withdraw our will's consent, the result will probably be a gradual descent into mediocrity, for God gives graces and lights so that we will take advantage of them. Though it may cause us deep suffering to stay open to his action, he will strengthen and uphold us till the purification is completed, and we become his perfect instruments for loving.

If we refuse the insight into truth and withdraw from its consequences, we are only postponing what must happen before we receive our wedding garment. We are condemning ourselves to purgatory after death. Worse, we cannot be sure we will not slide back into bad habits long renounced, a lukewarmness in which we shall lose much of what we gained through former purifications.

The imperishable glory of the Lord rising like the day star in our hearts will banish all our darknesses if we let it. Our passivity under its transfiguring influence has to be a conscious, deliberate opening of ourselves down to the deepest levels. This may well be the most arduous, agonizing effort of our whole lives, but the price paid is worth the heavenly gift bestowed.

John expresses it this way: "In the same way the will is informed with divine love, so that it is a will that is now no less than divine, nor does it love otherwise than divinely, for it is made and united in one with the divine will and love. So, too, is it with the memory; and likewise the affections and desires are all changed and converted divinely, according to God. And thus this soul will now be a soul of heaven, heavenly, and more divine than human. . . . God continues . . . illumining and enkindling it divinely with yearnings for God alone and for naught else whatsoever" (*D.N.* II,XIII,11).

Unfinished Business

There are oddments lying about
all over the place. I keep
tripping over them. My feet
get tangled up in yards of ribbon
—like shredded rainbows—we once used

for festive decorations. I stumble
over gifts of reverential love
we artlessly bestowed upon each other.
Sometimes I lurch and fall flat on my face
to lie there weeping in the muddle
of what was once
an ordered tranquil space for intermingling
spirit flowing into spirit
waterfalls in sunshine
lilies of the field that had no need
to toil and spin, but only to receive.

Bombs do this when let fall.
A careless devastation is their trademark.
Exploding, they wreck the spires of trust, delicate as lace,
wrought with such patient care, exactitude and pain
till they became that airy shrine
we entered, hand in hand, to pray.
It was you who made this mess.
You spoke those words of cold disintegration,
slashed the ties of mutual covenant
and wrenched that life-support contraption from its plug.

All I could do was shut the door behind me,
and walk away from you dry-eyed, pretending
that I did not care about the chaos
—unfinished business cluttering walls and floors—
in what was once our sanctuary
sacred as the consecrated bread
blessed by the Spirit's hovering Presence.

Our humanness betrayed us.
We wrecked our shrine together.

15 Purification of the Intellect

In the passive purgations the human intellect must learn to abdicate (in matters to do with the spiritual life) in favor of the Spirit's wisdom. Crucifixion of the intellect opens the way for divine wisdom to be infused into the understanding. We receive the intuitive, spiritual "knowing" that is beyond, yet does not falsify, or deny, reason. To attain this "knowing" we have to travel by way of faith through the cloud of unknowing which, John of the Cross tells us, is "thick darkness to the understanding."

The purpose and general effects of the night of faith have been examined in earlier chapters. Crucifixion of the intellect occurs at that point where the night's darkness is at its most impenetrable, absurd and excruciating. Here God is calling us to the ultimate renunciation of the "proprietary" use of our faculty of understanding.

The human intellect is a marvelous instrument that enables us to deal with those aspects of knowledge necessary for our life in the world. It can even probe many of the mysteries of existence, as the expositions of the great religions, philosophies and sciences show.

But it cannot penetrate the mysteries of the Trinity and its dealings with us human beings and our universe. It recoils baffled, unable to go beyond a certain point. Even Thomas Aquinas admitted he could not plumb the depths of God and had been shown more of them in one ecstatic union with the Spirit than in all his years of study and thought.

St. Paul affirmed the same discovery. "Who could ever know the mind of the Lord? Who could ever be his counsellor? Who could ever give him anything or lend him anything? All that exists comes from him; all is by him and for him" (Rom 11:34-36).

"The Spirit reaches the depths of everything, even the depths of God. After all, the depths of a man can only be known by his own spirit, not by any other and in the same way the depths of God can only be known by the Spirit of God" (1 Cor 2:10-11).

In spite of its limitations, the human intellect, being vulnerable to pride and arrogance, too often believes it knows better than God. Dazzled, we let it convince us that it alone is a sufficient guide to holiness and God's will for us.

However, Jesus himself nowhere said, "Be clever, and you will be holy and please the Father." Instead, he praised faith, love, obedience, humility, simplicity and devotion to the Father's will. It is the way outlined by him that we choose to follow when living out his passion, death and resurrection with him. We thus invite the Spirit to penetrate and transform our whole being, including our understanding.

Grace makes us aware that we need to become detached from the certainties and comforts of our own deeply rooted ideas and convictions about God and our spiritual life, even though these are providing us with the security of confinement in the known and comprehensible. Relinquishments of self-enclosure are acutely disturbing, and so is this one. To receive God in the fullness and manner that is his will for each of us entails a kind of mind-blowing experience that is the equivalent of crucifixion of the understanding on the cross of pure faith.

Those in the night of the spirit are no longer ruled or influenced by desire for material goods. Their temptations are more subtle and dangerous, being concerned with spiritual goods. If we are to walk in pure faith, we have to train ourselves to desire only that spirituality God wills to give us at the time and place and in the manner he chooses.

The effect of such purity of intention is to leave blanks in the memory and imagination. These are like sheets of paper on which we invite God to write whatever he wishes, and where the only word we ourselves inscribe is "Amen." "For who shall prevent God from doing that which he will in the soul that is resigned, annihilated and detached?" (*Ascent* II,IV,2).

The memory and imagination cannot be entirely quelled in relation to our spiritual life, and in certain kinds of temperament and intellect remain indefatigably active. The trick is not to identify with them. Disregard their antics, attach no importance to them, retire into the empty silence of faith and rest there in God's incomprehensibility.

Any kind of fixed ideas about God and the spiritual life, especially our own, are likely to be an entanglement, hindering further progress toward union. Many of them have evolved because they give spiritual, emotional or intellectual reassurance. It is always difficult to relinquish what helps us feel safe and at home. This is especially so for the emotionally insecure, who have a compulsion to cling to people, ideas and convictions that give security. All of us are insecure in one way or another, but for some this produces an anxiety so deep and intense it amounts to an affliction.

Such people need to know where they are, what is happening, where they are going, why and how things are the way they are and what they will probably become. This goes for both day-to-day and spiritual matters. Yet the fivefold *nada* involves not clinging to anything or anyone at all, except the Divine Being.

The cleverer the intellect and the more fragile the sense of security, the more we are tempted to rationalize until a tangle of interdependent concepts about the spiritual life and our position in it is formed. Its purpose is to protect the psyche from pain and shock. Unfortunately, it also impedes the Spirit's free penetration of the same psyche, so that divine wisdom and will cannot be implanted deep down where the springs of action have their source. A palisade of intellectual idols is in the way.

"To enter upon this road . . . is to leave one's own way, and to enter upon that which has no way, which is God. For the soul that attains to this state has no longer any ways or methods, still less is it attached to ways and methods, or is capable of being attached to them. I mean ways of understanding, or of perception, or of feeling. Nevertheless it has within itself all ways, after the way of one that possesses nothing, yet possesses all things. For, if it have courage to pass beyond its natural limitations, both interiorly and exteriorly, it enters within the limits of the supernatural, which has no way, yet in substance has all ways" (*Ascent* II,IV,5).

The roots of bad and imperfect habits can be uncovered only by means of the passive purifications. The vice-like hold of the intellect upon its possessions has to be broken, and breaking hurts. Yet the Spirit, though implacable, is also tender and healing. She can be trusted to bring about the purification in a way that will in the end lead to the soul's peace and wholeness, where free-floating anxiety becomes free-floating abandonment.

Whatever the cause of our entanglement in intellect, we have to attain the kind of detachment and purity of intention that enables us to relinquish willingly and immediately each concept as soon as the Spirit reveals its inadequacy. Then the clutter such ideas and attachments to them have caused in the understanding will be dissolved away to be replaced by simplicity and freedom. This is to have reached poverty of spirit.

The *Submit—Wait—Fast* program has relevance to both the active and passive aspects of the understanding's purification. It can be enlarged this way:

Submit to the confusion and muddle of:
  Not knowing
  Not understanding
  Not being right

Wait for the spirit to resolve it

Fast from the "richness"
  (emotional and intellectual security) of:
  Knowing
  Understanding
  Being Right

In the active night we use our wills to consent to the confusion and muddle, the sense of absurdity, that arise when the intellect's attempts to reason and understand become submerged in the thick darkness of faith. We learn to submit to all this by a process of "let be, let go, let God." The trials then persist on one level, while faith takes peaceful charge on another.

"For the less the soul works with its own ability, the more securely it journeys, because it journeys more in faith" (*Ascent* II,I,3).

"The less they understand, the farther they penetrate into the night of the spirit . . . through which they must pass in order to be united with God, in a union that transcends all knowledge" (*Ascent* II,XIV,4).

Faith wants to pervade the rational that knows, understands, seeks to be right, with the irrationality of the divine. God's ways are not our ways, and his justice is other than ours because he sees the whole as it is, whereas we see only disjointed snippets. He is calling us to use our will to oppose the urge and temptation to question and argue with him, asserting our own ideas of what is best to do about all this amorphousness and indefinability.

Genuine security is found in abandonment in darkness, not in feeling safe because we know and understand what is happening. The general rules could well be: Don't try to make it happen. Don't hope it will happen again. Don't attempt to interpret it or lead on from it to "the next stage." Just let it happen and let it stop happening. Float.

This entails checking the tendency to build up rational structures and maps from our past and present experience, decide (rationally) where they indicate we are heading, convince ourselves (rationally) this is God's will for us, and set about (rationally) facilitating our progress along that route.

God changes direction bewilderingly, and unless we keep our eyes on him and change accordingly, we shall be left behind with nothing but our cherished but now out of date maps, and no idea of how to apply them.

Caussade's most perceptive and interesting commentary on what he calls "the attachment to the spirit of self-ownership" has been dealt with in an earlier chapter. He continues by saying, "Divine love . . . wishes that the actual *manner* of attributing all to it should depend only on his divine choice, on his pure spirit and grace, with a continual dependence, not only in the interior acts of our powers but even in the *manner* of performing those acts; for often God wishes them to be exercised in one fashion and we in another" (*On Prayer*, pp. 251-252).

Discarding our maps means we are being summoned to an even more radical renunciation of attachment to the *manner* in which our adherence to his will is to be practiced. Such total surrender entails not only submitting in faith to all the ebbs and flows of the Spirit. It also means waiting in patience for God to act, while we fast from our urges and desires and plans to get moving and organize matters and "the manner of performing them" in the way that to our own understanding seems so obviously right.

Perfect union with God's will such as Caussade requires is never reached without immersion in the deepest passive purgations. This is where the true and agonizing crucifixion of the intellect occurs.

Crucifixion means annihilation of self-love and self-will. It involves naysaying right down to the depths, being crossed out as if one did not exist, having everything one cares about taken away while one remains powerless under the long, slow torture. Jesus on his cross is the archetype.

Crucifixion of the intellect involves the intensification of muddle, confusion and inability to understand when the need to feel safe and sure in our thinking is most urgent. It can provoke spasms of mental frenzy and thrashing about that, if prolonged, threaten madness.

In contrast, the action of grace in the depths can transport the intellect almost instantaneously from a state of inner turmoil to one of calm lucidity in which truths are infused, light is everywhere, and a delicate peace encompasses one's whole being. This is so obviously a gift from God that all one can do is humble oneself and give thanks for deliverance.

These violent swings themselves induce the fear of madness. To abandon oneself to divine providence in the midst of such fear requires heroism.

Whether our inner state is at either extreme, the remedy is a series of acts of abandonment as total as the will can make, based on the *Submit—Wait—Fast* program. We are passive; the Spirit is active. Let her act. Let the intellect be crucified in absurdity. The less we struggle, the less it hurts and the quicker it will be over.

When total inability to understand is reached, that is the cutoff point, the impasse. We cease trying to fathom what the Spirit is doing or accomplishing, or why, or how. This applies whether the action is taking place in prayer (non-prayer), personal relationships (crumbling and revealing hollowness), daily life (a series of negations and privations), acute interior sufferings (largely caused because we are being rigid rather than limp).

All these are the *means* and *manner* which the Spirit has chosen out of the totality of our life circumstances and patterns as the best for leading us to full union. They are all part of the death and rebirth process. We do not have to understand what is happening, we only need to accept and stay still while we let ourselves be moved as, when and where God chooses.

"The soul itself works . . . only by waiting upon God and by loving him without desiring to feel or see anything. Then God communicates himself to it passively, even as to one who has his eyes open, so that light is communicated to him passively without his doing more than keep them open. And this reception of light, which is infused supernaturally, is passive understanding" (*Ascent* II,XVI,2).

We have to avoid fiddling with the intellect when God wants it left alone so he can deal with it through the passive purgations. To fashion a concept in the understanding and then to want with the will what one has created is to disturb tranquillity and block receptivity. Abandonment is present when there is evidence in us of stillness, peace, enfoldment, love, freedom from desire, sublime knowledge (see *Ascent* II,XV,5). But it can also be present to a marked degree concealed under a surface turmoil that, for all its drama, has no power to shake the hidden depths of a will utterly consecrated to God and his purposes.

Tranquillity in the understanding comes when we accept that we cannot understand and are no longer troubled by this lack. The "cannot" is the cutoff point at which we are released into the thick darkness of pure faith and must leave everything to divine providence. Abandonment can be either crucifying or consoling.

"Learn to be empty of all things, inwardly and outwardly, and you will see that I am God" (*Ascent* II,XV,5).

All this is not to say that concepts, illuminations, messages, holy desires may not come directly, in peace, from the Spirit into the human mind and soul. What we have to remember is (1) they are delivered to a faulty receiving apparatus which, though with love and good will, may misinterpret or misapply them; (2) God may decide to fulfill them in a way other than we (correctly at the time) understand him to mean; and (3) this new way may be because of changed circumstances, or to better fulfill us, or to honor him and his will more gloriously, or to answer a developed capacity in us to respond more fully to his love, or to keep the fulfillment for us till after death, making it even more complete as a result of our patient and purgatorial waiting.

God's divine providence operates in and through everchanging human beings to whom he has given free will. He adapts his action accordingly. All the more reason why we must remain pliable and ready to renounce at any time our own limited understandings and spiritual desires based on them.

If we submit, wait and fast in this state, we shall not be dismayed when God's revelations to us personally are changed, altered, withdrawn, or not fulfilled in the way expected. He chooses the way and time, the how and when, the whether or not. We may speculate (detachedly!), but never have set ideas and convictions about the insights and inspirations given by the Spirit. She may infuse a deeper understanding when she knows we are capable of grasping it and opening ourselves to her will in the matter.

Readiness is all. The timing is crucial and not for us to choose. God permits no buts and ifs. The intellect is called to submit completely to the fact that he alone knows best, whereas we are tangled up in not knowing, not understanding and not being right.

"It is impossible to understand the hidden truths of God which are in his sayings, and the multitude of their meanings. He . . . speaks according to the way of eternity . . . we understand only the ways of flesh and time" (*Ascent* II,XX,5).

The solution for us is to be so abandoned that we float weightlessly in his will and in his wisdom as they exist in eternity and infinity, relinquishing the need to understand. This is freedom.

Such weightlessness is the result of jettisoning all fears, anxieties, clutchings for emotional and intellectual security, needs to know and understand, disturbances about not being right, humiliations at being wrong and making mistakes and being stupid, suffering and frustration over being denied what we had believed God had promised, dismay at absurdity, meaninglessness and contradictions in the divine action.

The floating in the divine will that is the result of such a crucifixion of the intellect could well be the true levitation, because it is purely spiritual and interior.

Some of the specific areas in which the Spirit will be active to remove impediments that prevent such free-floating of the understanding are:

1) *Delusions*. These are sincerely held and often obstinately so. Some people are gifted with a "natural facility" through which their "many tastes and affections and the operations of their faculties are fixed upon God and spiritual things." Because of this they think they are receiving "spiritual blessings" in a supernatural way when these arise only from their own natural capacities (see *D.N.* II,XVI,5).

The Spirit is working to produce a genuine transformation

where all spiritual blessings will originate from God and be infused into us by her own action. For this to happen, the gifts and graces we think up for ourselves and, as it were, bestow upon ourselves, while being convinced they come from God, have to be deprived of their force and power to convince, until "they have no more strength" (*D.N.* II,XVI,6).

"When the soul is making most progress, it is travelling in darkness, knowing naught" (*D.N.* II,XVI,8).

Delusions can be subtle and deep-seated. They are open to diabolic manipulation. The remedy is self-distrust and skepticism coupled with trust in God and guileless openness with one's director.

One of the chief works of the crucifixion of the intellect is to strip away all delusions, thus opening up the mind and emptying it of its attachments to distortions of the truth. Then Wisdom herself can enter and occupy the place God has prepared for her.

2) *Rationalizations*. These fulfill our personal want and need to be sure we are in the right, while they keep our consciences clear. A good name for them is "clever talk." When elaborate, they can form an efficient cover over dubious motives and self-indulgences, much as surface camouflage conceals the hideout of a nuclear missile.

Constructing rationalizations can keep the intellect so busy and preoccupied that faith and contemplation are inhibited. The rationalizer has a compulsion to be in the right and get his own way. This urge may be rooted in emotional insecurity yet one of the purposes of the passive purifications is to arouse and exacerbate such insecurities till we have no recourse but to turn them and our whole lives over to God.

Unconscious drives get in our way and in God's, trying to influence "the *manner* of our performance," yet because of their strength and concealment are beyond our power to locate and to eradicate. The only remedy is to be completely passive under the probings of divine action. Let God's "manner of performance" have center stage, while we wait in the wings.

Rationalizations comfort and reassure us that all is well, but God wants us to face the fact that, in spite of our sincere efforts, all is far from well. Besides this, they are a distortion, whether subtle or gross, of the truth of our relationship with God. They try to convince us, "I'm OK. I don't need you tampering with my life, God. I'm not doing anything wrong. My conscience is clear."

Our contribution, while waiting in the wings, could be a crafty "corner-the-rationalization" game—rather like catching lively fleas! However, as the darkness of the faith invasion encompasses the whole theater, we shall be unable to sight these lively distorters of the truth and will have to turn over to God both the entire stage performance and our own private pest eradication program.

3) *Ideals.* It may seem strange to suggest that part of our mental equipment that must be relinquished is our genuine ideals. Until the crucifixion of the intellect overtakes us, we do not realize we are trammelled by concepts derived from our human need, and that we have no proof that even the most precious and exalted of them has been implanted in us by the Spirit. Even if it has, we have inevitably warped it because our understanding is so limited and governed by the drive for self-fulfillment in the manner of our own choice.

Ideals may in the past have helped us to renounce the base and strive for the exalted. Their usefulness is over once we have entered the midnight of faith. Here they are ballast to be jettisoned.

Only God can choose for us what is to be our particular highest goal and fulfillment. Jesus is our ideal, but to idealize him is to put him beyond our reach, when the aim of his incarnation is to be like us in all things except sin and to stay closer to us than our own breath.

The process of idealization of other human beings, however good and even holy they may undeniably be, is always a distortion of the truth, for all goodness and holiness comes from God, and it is to him that the thanks and praise are due. "Why do you call me good? Only God is good," Jesus rebuked.

Ideals can also lead to immoderate commitment to and involvement in causes, consequent distortion of judgment and a lapse from devotion to God's will for itself alone. Rationalizations that we are doing his will, that this cause will therefore prosper and the ideal it holds out as its end aim be victorious, cover a variety of self-seekings and evasions of the truth.

In the passive purifications of the understanding the Spirit cleanses us from our ideals and idealizations through disillusionment, defeats, broken relationships, lost causes, betrayals and bleak self-insights.

4) *Fantasies*. Many great works of art have their origin in or are influenced by fantasy, and fantasy in its fun aspect can give delight to many. This is not the kind of use of the imagination that the passive purgations are aimed at.

The imagination and memory cling to the past, adorn the present, and construct scenarios for the future in relation to both our spiritual and daily lives. All of these are distortions of the truth, encrustations on the intellect marring the simplicity of faith and abandonment.

Harmful fantasies also arise from our own buried needs, lacks, compulsions and obsessions. We cannot let go because we need to be reassured. Seeking reassurance, we reconstruct the past so that it is more emotionally satisfying, or puts us more obviously in the right, or humiliates those who have belittled us, or shores up our lack of confidence by presenting defeat as disguised success.

Some fantasies of the past are played over and over like records stuck in a groove or repeat programs of low-grade films in a 24-hour movie theater.

We decorate the present by imposing our own interpretations and wish fulfillments on what is happening. We escape from facing it as it is by evasive action consisting of a series of sidesteps and backwards movements away from the bare truth. We imagine to be there what is not present, and let memories of the past interpose themselves between us and the actuality of the present moment.

Caussade stresses that the present moment is, or ought to be, a sacrament, because it is the only moment in time in which divine providence is wholly present to us. By the misuse of fantasy we befoul this sacrament and shut ourselves off from its blessings.

We cannot know the future, yet we persistently fantasize about it. We hook in memories of the past and decide the future will be an embellishment of these. If the memories are unpleasant and painful, we dread the future. If happy and fulfilled we disregard the reality of the present and project ourselves into an imagined, even more ecstatic scenario.

The degree of danger in all this is in proportion to its willfulness. If we struggle against deliberate consent to and indulgence in it, we show the Spirit we are inviting him to cleanse us passively of all such nonsense.

A genuine, profound love of and search for the truth as God sees it provides a powerful counterbalance to over-indulgence in a harmful use of memory and imagination in fantasy.

5) *Inner talking*. This is a common aspect of misuse of memory and imagination. Dialogues or long speeches of self-justification; endless repetitions of slogans; tags of approval or disapproval tied on us by others, or on them by us; grief-stricken reproaches; declarations of love; pleadings for understanding; angry accusations— these and many variations of them invade the mind like a swarm of insects that wheel and dart at whim.

Because often obsessive and compulsive, such invasions are difficult or impossible to control by will. The origin of their persistence is outside consciousness, though they may relate directly to remembered happenings and real people. A person hooked on them is apt to sit with a fixed, unblinking gaze, oblivious of real surroundings, absorbed in the inner drama.

Consciousness of what is happening and a deliberate effort to dissociate from it have to be cultivated by turning the mind to prayer or positive thinking (most inner talk is negative and destructive), or directing the attention outward. If this proves impossible, a dive deep underneath them into faith's thick darkness where God is, will soon make such vocal dramas irrelevant and quell their commotion.

In the night of the spirit this kind of activity of the memory and imagination is much more a trial and temptation, or even an affliction, than a deliberate fault. Through doggedly persisting in trying to detach ourselves, we grow in recollection of the will (which is the deepest recollection), in spite of lack of it in the mind. If we wait in abandonment for deliverance, the Spirit eventually infuses another kind of recollection where stillness invades all the faculties so all this nonsensical, unproductive inner talk simply ceases before awareness of God's presence.

6) *Patterns and maps*. We make these for ourselves in both useful and harmful ways.

A detached, clinical examination of our own life experience and our spiritual development, if prayerfully and humbly done, will usually reveal repetitive patterns. These indicate areas of weakness and strength, places where grace has been at work in, on and through us maybe for years, compulsive and obsessive syndromes of behavior harmful to spiritual development, blockages to growth evincing themselves in persistent disasters and setbacks that curiously resemble one another.

If such self-examinations are done not in morbid introspection (which is disguised self-love), but prayerfully in the Spirit, asking for enlightenment, they amount to meticulous examinations of conscience.

The danger is when we are so unaware of our behavior patterns, their nature and effects, that we let them unconsciously influence us into making life maps. Once these maps are drawn, we feel safe only when compulsively adhering to them. We become rigid and ossified. We grind to a halt spiritually and are closed to the Spirit's entry and her gifts of interior renewal.

If under all this God finds a will that truly longs for him but is powerless because of undeliberate hardening of the spiritual arteries (to vary the map metaphor), he may send the kind of grace that registers on us as cataclysmic. There is a mental or emotional collapse, a deviation into bizarre behavior, acute anxiety attacks, outbursts of passionate revolt—or some other totally unexpected upheavals.

Their effects on the psyche are like that of a scale six earthquake on landforms. It breaks up the established pattern of roads, fences, buildings, rivers, hills, valleys, and obliterates the familiar. Old routes are no longer operable, so new ones have to be found and followed.

This kind of happening can be part of the passive purgations of the understanding for some people. They are then in great need of spiritual support and expert guidance and reassurance from an experienced director.

7) *Projections*. These are figurative garments that we impose on other people, and even on God, and then treat the disguises as if they were the truth.

The garments really belong to us, but we prefer not to admit to ourselves that they do. We hide them away in dark, locked closets and repress all awareness of them. These aspects of ourselves may have been the cause of rejection, condemnation and cruelty toward us in our early childhood. We learned then that it was safer to hide them and act as if they did not exist.

However, these aspects retain a dangerous potency. We relieve inner pressure by clothing other people in our own hidden garments. Then we criticize and condemn them for their vile tempers, foul tongues, dirty minds, dishonest ways, meanness, self-centeredness, boasting, pharisaism—and so on.

In this way we castigate others for our own unfaced faults and sins. Wherever there is over-reaction, fanaticism, blanket condemnation, double standards and hypocrisy, we can suspect projection and repression, aided and abetted by misuse of the memory and imagination.

Jesus had clear insight into this problem when confronted with the woman taken in adultery by her self-righteous captors. He knew that secretly, deep in their own hearts and imaginations, they desired her sexually themselves, so he said "Let him who is without sin cast the first stone." It is to be assumed they stole away one by one because the Spirit momentarily gave each of them a humiliating glimpse of the fornicator's garment hidden in his own closet.

Thus their self-understanding received a true, though unwelcome enlargement. Projections are psychological, not intellectual phenomena, yet they warp our understanding of ourselves and others. It is through the intellect that the Spirit is going to give us knowledge of them as they surface in the course of the passive purifications.

With these painful self-insights, the Spirit will also offer the grace to face and accept them, but we have to muster the humility and courage to do so. If we react positively, we shall have absorbed a little more of divine wisdom, and in the self-knowledge given by it, be able to say, and mean it, "There but for the grace of God, go I," instead of imposing our own hidden garments upon others' reality.

8) *Jungian elements.* I should like to point out that much of what Jung says about the *persona,* the *shadow, archetypes, animus* and *anima, myth,* the *collective* and the *personal unconscious* has relevance to the themes of this chapter.

If our understanding of God, ourselves, others and life is to be purified, the unconscious elements within us have to be brought to the surface, especially if they are blocking our deeper union with the Trinity. As already noted in previous chapters, the passive purgations accomplish in the soul at least some of the work that a skilled psychotherapist would with a cooperative patient seeking truth. Both lead to an integration of the self.

Learning the nature of our own personal "shadow" and how to expose it to expert interpretation and healing so that it is finally incorporated creatively into our consciousness is the equivalent, on another level, of what grace accomplishes in relation to our spiritual life in the dark night.

Jung's own expositions in his collected works might be too complex and difficult for many to profit from them, but his ideas have been popularized by a number of writers.

As a final comment on this chapter, I stress that in all transactions between the Spirit and our spiritually ailing selves, a wise, patient, kind but implacable confessor-director is invaluable. The more learned he is, the better.

Once we can frankly present in the confessional the reprehensible element we have concealed within ourselves for so long, we are released to open ourselves even more to the divine invasion, welcoming instead of fearing it. Such a process is crucifying to self-love and should take place stage by stage as we grow strong enough in grace to receive it. To force the procedure is to try to impose upon God our own ideas of the how and when and the manner of his dealing with us. It is also to risk a breakdown.

Purification of the understanding entails the exposure and casting out of all lies we are living both in regard to ourselves and to others. The mechanisms detailed above belong among those lies, but as they are usually props to the insecure, they must not be removed until grace has given the inner strength to withstand the shocks entailed. That is why such deeper purifications take place in the night of the spirit when the soul is already advanced in grace, prayer and virtue.

St. John of the Cross sums it up best:

"The darkness which the soul here describes relates to the desires and faculties, sensual, interior and spiritual, for all these are darkened in this night as to their natural light, so that, being purged in this respect, they may be illumined with respect to the supernatural. For the spiritual and the sensual desires are put to sleep and mortified, so that they can experience nothing, either divine or human; the affections of the soul are oppressed and constrained, so that they can neither move nor find support in anything; the imagination is bound and can make no useful reflection; the memory is gone; the understanding is in darkness, unable to understand anything; and hence the will is likewise arid and constrained and all the faculties void and useless; and in addition to all this a thick and heavy cloud is upon the soul, keeping it in affliction, and, as it were, far away from God. It is in this kind of 'darkness' that the soul says it travelled 'securely.' . . .

"This (darkness) emanates from the dark light of wisdom. For in such a way does this dark night of contemplation absorb and immerse the soul in itself, and so near does it bring the soul to God, that it protects and delivers it from all that is not God. For this soul is now undergoing a cure, in order that it may regain its health—its health being God himself. His Majesty restricts it to a diet and abstinence from all things, and takes away its appetite for them all" (*D.N.* II,XVI,1 & 10).

The Brink

1

Eve
I know you hate me trying to teach you anything,
you stubborn, self-willed, mettlesome filly!
I know you think you know far more than I do,
that your primeval wisdom outranks my cultivated,
discriminating knowledge, that your intuitions
probe far more accurately, expose more pitilessly
than all my clever talk and cerebral pronouncements.

Maybe you're right. I often lose an argument with you.
But, Eve, couldn't it be both-and
instead of this unyielding either-or?

2

Eve
do you understand this ambivalent matter of faith?
No. Of course you don't. Your faith
is of the sinews and the blood, the womb's clutch,
the bondslave heart's compulsive drumbeat.

Eve
I understand you, sister twin.
I too have known captivity by those blood wisdoms,
the ancient rhythms ululating soundlessly within.

Eve
I need you to support me, give instructions
about primordial genius concealed
in vein and artery. I'm waiting for you to quench
this cerebral activity with all its buts and whys
and teach me once again to lie quiescent
in the wordless dark, letting the flood
bear me forward unresisting to the chasm's brink
where I will slide into the void of faith.

16 The Incurable Wound

SCRIPTURE SPEAKS OF an incurable wound in a number of places, for example: "I despair for this wound of mine! My injury is incurable!" (Jer 10:19); "Why is my suffering continual, my wound incurable, refusing to be healed?" (Jer 15:18); "And though I have not sinned, my wounds are incurable" (Job 34:6).

Sometimes the reference is to a person, at other times to Israel as a nation. The individual is often innocent, yet God has smitten him. Israel is usually guilty of whoring after strange gods, yet Yahweh longs only for her to repent and return to the enfoldment of his yearning love.

In Isaiah we find the Suffering Servant, who, innocent in every way, is made a scapegoat for the people, despised, forsaken, physically attacked by them, wounded in heart and body, bearing their sins for them.

These Old Testament innocent victims, with their incurable wounds, remind us of Jesus, innocent yet "made sin" for us. Rejected and reviled by the very ones he came to save, and experiencing himself as forsaken even by God, he suffered what we term "a broken heart," an interior wound externalized at the piercing of his side by the soldier's lance in the coup de grace.

The risen, glorified body of Christ bears his five wounds for eternity. The wound in his heart remains incurable in the sense that his continuous passion and extended incarnation are perpetuated throughout his mystical body, the church—that means in us, the members of his body.

Our incurable wound is twofold. First, it consists of the wound of sin shared by all humanity from the beginning of its creation to the parousia. The first syndrome is the result of this primeval wound.

Second, it exists in the mystical body of Christ as it continues his

153

redemptive work in the world and time in the second syndrome. Christ no longer suffers in his glorified, heavenly state, but he has chosen to be so merged with us that he continues to do so in us, with us, for us, existentially, where we are, now.

This wound in us is incurable in that the willing must suffer for the unwilling, as surrogates, till human beings and sin together vacate this earth.

The wounded heart of Jesus has held special mystical, symbolic meaning ever since the church's earliest days. When it was pierced, the water that flowed out was held to symbolize baptism, and the blood, the Eucharist. It was the church herself that was born from Christ's incurable wound by water and by blood. Thus the baptized automatically participate in the sacrament of salvation for the whole world.

Whether aware of it or not, they are included in his redemptive act. They have the choice of deliberately agreeing to share his sufferings with him, or dissociating themselves from him. For the sharers, their suffering is their love and their love is their suffering, for the disciples are not greater than the Master, and the total gift of self means total involvement in his destiny.

During the passive purgations the hearts of those who have given themselves to Jesus are sharing intimately in his passion, and so coming to resemble his heart. Its wounds and flow of blood and water are for them the source and sign of the Lord's infinite, sacrificial, redeeming love, which they are invited to absorb into their own hearts and use to love others with.

At the Last Supper, Jesus commanded the disciples to love one another in the same way he had loved them. This can be done only by giving one's heart to him, thus initiating the long process of purgation which will bear with especial force and significance the characteristics of suffering and love. The culmination will be sharing in the crucifixion of Jesus and the piercing of his heart during the darkness of the night of the spirit and the passive purgations.

Jesus' flesh was real flesh, his love real love. The heart symbolizes our affective powers, and the heart of Jesus reminds us he was truly human, loving us with a perfect human love that was all God's divine, indestructible love, for in the Son the Father was made manifest. In the human love of this heart we recognize what we ourselves feel and express, our own tenderness, joy, grief, teasing,

humor, reproach, forgiveness, reaching out, hurt at rejection, longing for union. His love is so like ours, and yet so different.

The difference is awesome. Nowhere in Jesus' loving is there
any element of self-interest, meanness, pettiness, spite, revenge,
cruelty, fickleness, egoism, possessiveness, addiction, selfishness.
His human love is perfect. It throws into painful, humbling relief
all the imperfections and insufficiencies in our own way of loving.
And yet he has commanded us to love one another in the same kind
of way as he loves us. How can we ever be able to do this?

As we consider this conundrum, we realize that a total transformation of our affective powers, our hearts, has to take place. This is
why the passive purgations are so much concerned with purifying
the emotions. For the human heart to be lifted up and relocated in
the heart of Jesus, so it can love with his love, there must be an interior crucifixion of self-love, self-will and self-interest. According to
the usual paradoxes of the passive purgations, this means death and
rebirth, destruction of one's old self and its renewal and reconstruction in a new, Christed self.

Such a heart does not cease to be itself with its own individual
characteristics and potentialities, for grace does not destroy nature
but builds on and perfects it. The process feels like a long, slow, agonizing death. It will be years probably before the renewed heart begins to throb with the love of Jesus in any way that we are aware of
and so can derive consolation from.

"See, I have branded you on the palms of my hands" (Is 49:16),
Jesus says, holding out his nailed hands to us to welcome us. He also
points to the wound in his heart, and instead of saying as he did to
Thomas, "Thrust in your hand," he says, "Thrust in your whole
self, for through this place you pass into heaven with me."

The purgatorial journey of the passive purifications is a passage
through the sacred heart, which at the end is inseparably blended
with ours in spiritual marriage. John, writing of the death of Jesus,
which was certified, as it were, by the thrusting spear, links it up
with the death to self in the spiritual purgations, and the effect this
has on others.

"It is certain that, at the moment of his death, he was likewise
annihilated in his soul, and was deprived of any relief and consolation, since his Father left him in the most intense aridity, according
to the lower part of his nature. And thus he wrought herein the

greatest work that he had ever wrought . . . at the moment and the time when he was most completely annihilated in everything" (*Ascent* II,VII,11).

This "greatest work" was the salvation of the whole world, which he extends through his body, the church, enabling us to participate in it with him. Those who give him their hearts to love and suffer in for his redemptive work thus help change the course of history. They also agree to be afflicted with his incurable wound and to bear its suffering with him for others.

The incurable wound in the human heart comes from four sources of interior suffering: mental, psychological, emotional and spiritual. Mostly, a mixture of these is evident, with one predominating at any particular time. The passive purgations tend to be holistic.

The concentrated form that culminates in the crucifixion of the heart consists especially in a sense of total rejection by God and humans. This is epitomized in our Lord's cry to his Father, "My God, my God, why have you forsaken me?" The heart feels finally deserted by God in whom it had placed its total trust. It hears all about it a jeering and mocking that seems diabolically malicious and cruel. "He relied on Yahweh, let Yahweh save him! / If Yahweh is his friend, let Him rescue him!" (Ps 22:8).

Every time it makes an act of faith, trust, hope, or anguished love, the inward cackling, hideous laughter and evil tongues tear it to shreds. They proclaim that God does not hear or care, that he is deaf, blind and dumb. Because he permits this faithful servant to go down into the pit alive, while he refuses the help his almighty power could give at any moment, he cannot be a God of love and mercy. He must be some kind of soulless shredding machine, foreknowing and planning what would happen to his servant so he could gloat over her dereliction.

The heart experiences God as a darksome, devouring beast of prey (cf. Lamentations). It feels as if pincers are fastened in it, wrenching it this way and that. All the aspects of excruciating physical suffering are present in a metaphysical sense. Reference to them is the only way it can express what is happening interiorly. In its torture it may fear it is blaspheming against God, and this adds to its agony. However, it is actually making a continuous series of direct acts which are the exact contrary to the violent feelings and images flooding it.

Direct acts occur in the hidden depths of a heart given up to Jesus for him to love and suffer in, when the intensity of the passive purgations blot out all awareness of God's presence and his consolations. They are the spontaneous, involuntary affirmations of trust, love and hope that for decades the heart has trained itself to offer God under all circumstances, and which now continue of themselves when the anguish of rejection destroys the ability to make them consciously.

Mostly the heart is oblivious of these direct acts, and this, of course, increases its suffering. To love God and to be incapable of expressing that love, as if bound, gagged and incarcerated, is an exquisite form of torture. Yet, paradoxically, the heart's total impotence registers upon God as total faithfulness to him and his will for its purification. There is no failure or lapse or loss of intensity in its loving devotion. Its very condition of crucifixion is the expression of heroic obedience and love.

God never forsakes it, nor could or would he. It lacks the grace of awareness of anything but the negative aspects of its condition, but what is happening in these is all the time feeding, strengthening and spiritualizing its affective powers. Its ceaseless flow of secret, spontaneous, direct acts continually give the highest kind of honor and glory to God, who himself never ceases cherishing it.

"Christ redeemed us from the curse of the Law by being cursed for our sake" (Gal 3:13). The heart is experiencing, in union with Jesus, the anguish of being cursed and spurned. An essential component of the incurable wound is this sense of being cursed, not blessed. This is what Jesus endured on the cross when he took our place and was condemned instead of us so we could enter into the blessing and wholeness of God.

All through the Old Testament God alternately blessed and cursed Israel. Job and Jeremiah and other great figures personally endured the extremes of this repetitive cycle. It is part of the human condition, of our erratic progress toward completion in God, of the necessary oscillations of darkness and light in our interior purification.

Scripture threatens the curse can become absolute and eternal if we die in our sins. The result would be total, unceasing alienation from God. On the cross Jesus let himself be immersed in that damnation of forsakenness, except for the uttermost fastness of his will where he and the Father remained one and could never be separated.

He let himself plummet into hell to save us from that fate. He was "annihilated in his soul" and "in everything" (*Ascent* II,VII,11) to do with his humanity and his work of sin-taking. The heart given for him to love and suffer in lets itself be sucked into this whirlpool of alienation and cursedness in order to share in his redemptive work, saving souls with him for the kingdom. The reality of this inner experience of being cursed is awful past telling, yet its effects are wholly and gloriously positive. Through it the incurable wound in the heart of humanity is cured.

From the depths of his wounding, Jesus cried out, "I thirst!" This could mean physical thirst only, or this plus intolerable thirst for the salvation of the whole world, or us in him thirsting for God and our fulfillment in him, or a dreadful thirst for love from us and from the Father, or a consuming spiritual aridity in his absolute desolation of the senses and absence of any feeling that he was loved and cherished. Or it could mean a combination of all these.

The cry is echoed in our own hearts as we endure the passive purgations and the crucifixion with him, longing for our sufferings to be part of the church's vocation as the sacrament of salvation for the whole world.

His posture on the cross is one of total openness to God's action. He has no barriers or shields against the cruelties hurled at him. He is a sinless victim of devastating vulnerability. The heart that is one with him also experiences itself as defenseless in its confrontation with God and humanity. It is as naked as Jesus crucified. There is no one to defend it or save it from mockery, hatred, humiliation, repudiation—blow after blow, till it feels flayed.

> "Deep is calling to deep
> as your cataracts roar;
> All your waves, your breakers, have rolled over me"
> (Ps 42:7).

The depths of the human heart call upon the depths of the sacred heart for comfort and reassurance, but these are obliterated in the roar of the storm of destructive wrath raging about them both.

Only such a total immersion can make up for sin and result in final cleansing.

In the end, suffering becomes congealed. It sets like concrete in the heart and is carried about all the time as a weight threatening to bear us down finally into the pit of the lost. Only grace and God's power can dissolve it away, and grace will come only when the Sanctifier chooses, in the way he chooses, and usually without any feeling of consolation at this particular period.

We reach, with Jesus, the extremes of abandonment and can pray acceptingly, though in this pit of alienation, "It is accomplished" and "Father, into your hands I commend my spirit."

In this act of final, complete abandonment, the Servant of Salvation and his fellow servants, the one Victim heart and his companion human hearts, reach a strange, barren yet profoundly fulfilling sense of achievement. It is as if God is speaking through his Spirit in the farthest, inaccessible depth of the heart, using words from scripture:

> "You are my servant,
> I have chosen you, not rejected you;
> do not be afraid, for I am with you. . . .
> I am your God.
> I give you strength.
> I bring you help. I uphold you with my victorious
>   right hand" (Is 41:9-10).
> "I did forsake you for a brief moment,
> but with great love will take you back.
> In excess of anger, for a moment
> I hid my face from you.
> But with everlasting love I have taken pity on you,
> says Yahweh, your redeemer" (Is 54:7-8).

In what appears the finality of total defeat, Jesus has gotten himself the victory, and the wounded heart is sharing in his triumph. All wounds are about to be transfigured in his. The destiny of the sacred heart was to be broken for our salvation. The human hearts that have given themselves to him and been servants of salvation with him are about to experience the love that takes pity on them and heals all wounds.

The church is to be born in the outflow of blood and water, born already redeemed by the suffering hearts of the Lord and his servants.

"Gethsemane was witness to the conflict between the purity of God and the sin of the world, waged in the sacred humanity of Christ, who bore that twofold weight. In his humanity, he was crushed by it, broken, made into nothingness. . . . And yet the redemption of mankind, the birth and growth of the church have revealed the stature of the victory won in that combat by the patient Christ. The dark night of the spirit is a participation in that suffering and that victory" (Fr. Marie-Eugene, *I Am a Daughter of the Church*, p. 307).

Those who go down into the pit with Jesus out of love for him and neighbor and endure the passive purgations to their ultimate pang are destined to rise with him into the fullness of the new life of grace. Soon it will be time.

The Wound

Turn back the skin and the wound's
red mouth gapes "No!" repudiating both
the surgeon's scalpel and the casual, curious goad.
Exposure provokes throb and beat—
an atavistic music that could be
for dance or war, or parody of rhythmic love.

The wound is ululating now, indifferent
to ear compelled to listen and record
such archaic outcry. Thus keens
the abandoned child beating the cold breast
of its ravished mother's corpse, the screaming torch
the fire bomb ignited.
                        The putrifying leper,
the mutilated prisoner, moans like this—
the captured Jew, the unwed girl in labor,
the lover lonely on his empty bed, the young wife
with husband drowned a thousand miles from shore.

The theme is an old one that Eve made
when first her Adam struck her on the mouth
then went out into the sparse harvest
leaving her alone, her hand on her swollen womb,
a vision glazing her eyes of Adam, her man,
become Man, the red mouth of the wound
speared in his side retching a parched "Yes!"—
    wide open, inviting goad and scalpel.

Eve gasped. Her labor had begun.

17 The Sepulchre of Dark Death

THE ULTIMATE IN passivity is a corpse-like abandonment. This occurs when a complete impasse has been reached in our personal life, interior and exterior. All that one could do has been done and now one is impotent to do anything more. This state is symbolized by the entombment of Jesus.

"For in this sepulchre of dark death (the soul) must needs abide until the spiritual resurrection which it hopes for" (D.N. II,VI,1). In a sense all the passive purgations have been an entombment, but the deepest one occurs in a darkness and helplessness more intense than any preceding it. It has an air of crushing finality about it.

After his desolation on the cross, Jesus suffers the ultimate *kenosis* and dies. His death is real. The soldier's lance verifies that. The totality of the spiritual life requires that, after dying a spiritual death with and in him, we enter the tomb with and in him, lie down on the cold stone slab, and submit to *rigor mortis*—in our case not of the body, but of the heart and soul.

Ever since we gave ourselves to God, the grains of wheat of our selfishness have been falling into the ground of grace, dying there and taking on a new life of self-giving love. Ever deeper detachment and abandonment have led progressively to a more complete fulfillment of our baptismal initiation into Christ and his action within us. This has culminated in being crucified with him. The next phase is our share in his total *kenosis* and entombment.

For human beings there is no greater passivity and abandonment than death itself. That state brings about an involuntary, corpse-like obedience. In mystical death the same degree of obedience and abandonment to divine providence is called for, but it must be a voluntary acceptance of a spiritual state rather than of bodily death.

Through this mystical death, entombment, and rebirth into Christ's resurrection life, we shall finally enter spiritual marriage.

St. John teaches that this process is purgatory proper. Its severity is in direct relation to the degree of unitive love to which God intends to resurrect us. God is no more. He has died within us. We would be atheists, if we were not so deep-dyed in stubborn faith.

What did entombment mean for Jesus? What does it mean for us as members of his extended incarnation and continuous passion?

We are likely to experience some or all of the following:

1) *Real inner death.* In physical death we shall have no alternative but to relinquish everything and pass into another state of being where we shall see ourselves as God sees us and see God as he is. We shall undergo a devastating encounter with Truth, and there will be no way of evading it.

In mystical death something similar happens, but we still could choose to withdraw even at this late stage of involvement with Jesus. However, the fact that our will is completely captive in God's will makes such a withdrawal most improbable. It would amount to a violation of oneself.

God's will feels like a vice, closed tight about us, implacably pressuring us into immobility. We can do nothing to escape from the situation or even modify it. All we can do to survive is stay where God has placed us, and submit totally.

"God requires you to do nothing except to lie still and peacefully in your bonds and helplessness. . . . Let God handle you as though you were a dead body that can be manipulated, turned this way and that at will" (Caussade, *Self-abandonment to Divine Providence,* pp. 409-410).

It is worth remembering, when in this state, that the fullest possible union with God consists of a union of wills, not feelings. This spiritual death is the final expunging of self-will and its total fusion with the divine will. We have striven heroically to do our part. Now our role is to lie still and let God act in this most completely passive of the passive purgations. Here St. Francis de Sales' "Desire nothing, ask nothing, refuse nothing," acquires deeper and deeper significance for us.

We have been crossed out, taken off the record, made non-

persons. Only a smudge of suffering laid here in the tomb of abandonment remains. This is the extreme of poverty of spirit. If we endure to the end, we shall surely enter the kingdom of heaven and see
God.

Because it is human nature to organize our own lives and follow
our own wills, this enforced inactivity and complete negation register as death—which they are, the death of self-love, self-will, self-
interest, self-ownership. Now at last we say to God, "Do whatever
you like with me. I belong to you," and mean it to a fullness never
before achieved.

As the purifications deepen in the tomb, we see how incomplete
has been our abandonment in the past, in spite of all our sincerity
and renunciations. The self-ownership in our depths still grips like a
guard dog the last elements of the I AM and the I WANT, and even
now refuses to let go. Glimpsing it every now and then, perceiving
our helplessness before it, willing it to be erased, we make yet another and deeper act of submission, thus enabling God to do what
must be done.

We are consumed by the hunger to die to all that is not-God in
order to be fully alive in and for Christ.

2) *The non-prayer of the tomb.* In this state prayer becomes
nothing but a dumb, exhausted allegiance of the will, made in one
silent, painful, continuous effort with the last of our strength.

Entombment comes after the worst possible thing that could
happen to us has happened. It comes when our life is in ruins, our
hopes destroyed, our heart broken, our whole being cast into the
dark pit. Psalm 88 tells of this state.

> For my soul is all troubled,
> my life is on the brink of Sheol;
> I am numbered among those who go down to the Pit,
> a man bereft of strength:
>
> A man alone, down among the dead,
> among the slaughtered in their graves,
> among those you have forgotten,
> those deprived of your protecting hand.
>
> You have plunged me to the bottom of the Pit,

to its darkest, deepest place,
weighted down by your anger,
drowned beneath your waves.

You have turned my friends against me
and made me repulsive to them;
in prison and unable to escape,
my eyes are worn out with suffering (Ps 88:3-9).

There is no point in petitionary prayer, for we have grown accustomed to the one implacable answer, "Nothing for you." It has been like going day after day to the post office, asking, "Are there any letters for me?" and always receiving the same reply, "Nothing for you."

Yet faith idiotically persists in believing that God's "nothing" is also his "everything." In our numbness and dumbness he will reveal that to us. "When God does not give us what we wish, it is in order to give us what we would love more, if we knew all things" (St. Augustine, *Confessions*, V, VIII).

To keep stillness and silence, not wanting or asking anything, is what he requires of us in the tomb. The limpness of a totally acquiescent will, exhausted yet indomitable, provokes no desire to question God and no urge to rebel against his ways. All that is past. His ways are now accepted as totally incomprehensible. The only thing to do is to say nothing and let him carry out his plan. We have given up trying to understand what it is.

John's fivefold *nada*, the necessary nothingness of self-will's obliteration, silences all protestations and self-justifications. God is always and inevitably right. Has he not proved this over and over to us? Of course he has, and we know it. The injunction, "Be still, and know that I am God," takes on a new depth of meaning.

Our former facile spate of words has dried up. Our non-prayer is located somewhere deep in the crucified will that says nothing, but simply is in the midst of God's terrible, annihilating I AM. "I am the only self-subsistent Being. You are entirely contingent upon me. Why not face up to the truth and accept it?"

Some truths can be incorporated into one's being only in silence. The proud, wilful, primitive I AM of the ungraced self has given way to what seems a complete loss of selfhood. We feel stripped, defenseless, despoiled, made into a nothing, a no-thing. Our once mighty I AM is now only a faint chirping in the dust. There is in this state nothing to parade before God in order to impress him. He has reduced us to silence.

God said, "I am who I am." Our only prayer is now a crushed affirmation that he is, and all we can say of ourselves is, "And I am who I am." Having been clearly shown the truth, we crouch there, chastened, docile, tractable.

"When, with the help of grace, we have reached the stage of finding self intolerable and of knowing not the smallest satisfaction in our good works, our one remaining need is to endure that self with sweetness and to show it the same charity that it is our duty to show our neighbour" (Caussade, *Self-abandonment to Divine Providence*, p. 412).

Numb and speechless in the tomb, we learn to embrace the leper in ourselves in pity and acceptance, knowing that in his infinite compassion God himself loves and enfolds us just as we are. We shall grow into final wholeness not by repudiating this part of ourselves, but by facing facts. "This thing of darkness I acknowledge mine." We hold it up dumbly to the Spirit's renewing power.

The non-prayer of the tomb is essentially a simple laying open of our most impenetrable depths to divine providence. There are no secrets, no hiding places left. All is known. All is acknowledged. Our only hope is God's mercy.

Submit—Wait—Fast.

3) *Advent longing.* "Maranatha. Come, Lord Jesus, come." When our prayer is a total longing of our whole being for the Lord's advent, then he will come and lift us up into his own resurrection.

In the tomb there is no light. We are starved for light, but must come to the point of knowing it is the Light of the World that we long for, the Uncreated through whom all things were made, the Light that shines in the dark of the inner self and which the darkness cannot overpower, the one true Light that enlightens us all, and without whom the tomb's stygian blackness would be the only reality.

The abyss of darkness within us aches to be penetrated by the light. We want the totality of light, to be irradiated through and through, for in our poverty we have nothing to hide. Our Eve-Adam knows it is naked and only God can clothe it. It has given up all its fig-leaf dramas, and cries out to its Creator, "Come and clothe me with your righteousness. Cover me with Christ. Let him be my wedding garment." The vacuum left by the casting out of the last of self-will is drawing God into it.

"Let Israel wait for the Lord." But the whole of humanity, ever since that primordial catastrophe of mistaken direction, has been waiting and longing for the coming of the Lord.

> From the depths I call to you, Yahweh,
> Lord, listen to my cry for help!
> Listen compassionately
> to my pleading.
>
> I wait for Yahweh, my soul waits for him,
> I rely on his promise,
> my soul relies on the Lord
> more than a watchman on the coming of the dawn.
> (Ps 130)

In the liturgy this has traditionally been the psalm applied to the souls in purgatory, who are helpless to do anything at all but long and wait for Jesus to come to them and lift them up into glory. Those in purgatory in this life are in a similar state, but because they make a deliberate choice to be and remain in it, they are growing in holiness all the time. The more severe their trial, the more radiant they will shine when the time comes for the Light to lighten their darkness.

The immense longing for this advent arises from the inner emptiness made by the abdication of all attachments except that to God and his will. We neither cling to any of our former beloveds—persons or things—nor regard them as worth clinging to. We have let them all plunge into the depths of the Sacred Heart where divine love will enfold and take care of them, apportioning each to its right place whether within our hearts too or elsewhere. Either way it does not matter to us as long as Love's will is done. When Love himself knows it is the right time, they will be restored, sanctified, to us. But we are not longing for this restoration; we are longing for God himself.

"God, you are my God, I am seeking you,

> my soul is thirsting for you,
> my flesh is longing for you,
> a land parched, weary and waterless;
> I long to gaze on you in the sanctuary
> and to see your power and glory (Ps 63:1-2).

The whole of scripture is the account of this unquenchable, though hidden or disguised or misdirected, longing of the human heart for the advent of God. Often it is personified in Israel, the chosen of God, yet faithless, idolatrous, rebellious, straying, again and again. Through the prophets God calls his people home to him and continues to do so up to this present moment.

When the world has passed away through the privations of the active and passive nights, God's voice calling us home is no longer muffled and distorted like a radio station overlaid by other stations or constantly interrupted by static. His voice comes loud, clear and compelling.

Once we are in the tomb his voice echoes round the bare stone walls and empty space till it is magnified so painfully we can concentrate on nothing else.

The cry of our own hearts, "Come, Lord Jesus. Come," is answered by his reverberating summons, "Come to me, all you who are weary and heavy-laden and I will refresh you. Come all who are thirsty, and I will give you drink. Come all you wounded, and I will heal you. Come all you starved for love, and I will love you endlessly and infinitely. Come you lonely, and I will enfold you in my heart's wound. Come, my little ones, for I have prepared a place for you."

As his voice and words grow clearer, our waiting and longing become intolerable, and once there is nothing at all in us but this wound of waiting, he will claim us.

"When the Lord has given you the bread of suffering and the water of distress, he who is your teacher will hide no longer, and you will see your teacher with your own eyes" (Is 30:20).

4) *Loneliness.* In the tomb we exist in an all-enveloping loneliness. Only through a completely arid faith can we make contact with God. Our sensibilities have been mercilessly numbed by all we have been through. The coup de grace to the heart was given

when the worst possible thing that could happen to us, did happen.

We have been left in a queer state of dissociation from all living beings, including God. Our former way of loving, so laced with various kinds of selfishness and egoism, of which we were largely unaware till the passive purgations revealed them to us, has become impossible to us. The new way of loving as nothing but channels for Christ's love has not yet been perfected in us.

We long to relate deeply and truly to God and to the old or new beloveds, but somehow we do not have the psychological, emotional and spiritual means of making contact. Afraid of falling back into our old, flawed ways of loving, we remain limp and lifeless in our affectivity, waiting for the Spirit to take it over and lead us in a plain path where we walk in the strength and sureness of her love infused into us.

The chill of entombment has invaded our hearts. We long to love, but feel we have nothing to give. "There's nothing there," we tell ourselves despairingly. Helpless, poverty-stricken, frozen, desolate, we lie down in loneliness and decide this is to be our state until we die, for God has chosen it for us. We certainly did not choose it for ourselves.

Unable to believe in God's love, we yet go on believing. Unable to hope for rescue and new life, we yet go on hoping. Unable to love God or neighbor, we yet go on helplessly loving. All this is idiotic, yet it is the way things are with us.

We feel an intense aversion for our state, and even for God. In reality, this is an aversion against a return to our old ways of loving, the games we all unawares were playing, the dicing and the bargaining, the trading and the reservations, the subtle betrayals and the concealed self-indulgences. A red light goes on when we think we will reach out to some beloved, or even to God, for we now mistrust ourselves totally.

Something or Someone always warns us, "It's not the right time yet. . . . Wait a while longer. . . . You must go on waiting. . . . Submit to loneliness and let it do its work. . . . Rest in God's will and its choice of poverty, emptiness and despoliation for you. . . . Kiss the crucifix, and be still."

Caussade comforts, "You feel yourself to be without faith, hope or charity: this is because God deprives you of all perception of these virtues by making them abide in the higher part of the soul. In this way he puts you in a position of making a complete sacrifice of all your satisfaction, and there is surely nothing better than that. What, then, is your complaint? It comes of the fact that disconsolate humanity cries out against experiencing nothing but griefs, aridities and interior anguish. To the human element in you these are death-dealing, yet that human element has to die before you may receive the life of grace—that life which is altogether blessed and wholly divine" (*Self-abandonment to Divine Providence*, p. 413).

Paradoxically, the human element in us, the Eve/Adam, has to pass away before we can become truly human in the way God had in mind when he created us. To be fully, truly human is to be like Christ is in his humanity. We are caught in the limbo between what we were and are no longer, and what we are about to become but have not yet attained.

Loneliness of a particularly searing kind is inevitable, for we belong nowhere. All we know is that we feel cut off from God, the world and everyone else, and when we reach out a hand in the frozen darkness, there is no one there to clasp it.

Yet this very loneliness is the certain promise of future fulfillment of a transcendent, unimaginable delicacy and joy. If only we can lie down in it and wait without the least struggle or resistance, we will shorten the time, the stone will be rolled away sooner, and there in the dawn will be the risen Lord waiting with open arms.

5) *Indifference.* Indifference pervades one's being. Whether this is "holy" indifference we do not know. All we are sure of is that we want to say, wearily, submissively, sadly (but never defiantly, bitterly, angrily), about everyone and everything, "I don't care."

It is as if all ability to care has been beaten out of us, as sugar is crushed out of the cane, or water out of washed clothes put through a wringer.

Occasionally this not-caring is suffused with a kind of gentle holiness and we are sure, then, that it is a grace from God, a gift of detachment to reassure us. Mostly, in our numbness and dumbness, we exist in an unpleasant lethargy, as if our indifference is not holy, but the product of being forced into unwilling submission.

In accounts of torture, it is sometimes noted that the tortured person seems to become bored at a certain stage, shutting off and not reacting any longer.

Accidie? Lukewarmness? Or ecstatic detachment? (If ecstasy can be arid!)

Again, Caussade: "The proof and indication of death to all exterior things is a kind of indifference, or rather of insensibility, to all exterior goods, pleasures, reputation, relatives, friends and so forth. With the help of grace, such insensibility becomes so complete and so profound that we are tempted to believe it purely natural, and this God permits to safeguard us from any return of complacency and to enable us to go forward in all things in the obscurity of faith and a greater self-abandonment" (*Self-abandonment to Divine Providence*, pp. 423-424).

We feel this kind of indifference is somehow unclean, that we should be feeling something for others and be emotionally involved, yet if our neighbor is in need or our beloved calls out for help, we are the first there and spend ourselves recklessly—only we get no satisfaction from it.

Indifference has become the antidote to the vehement and often self-centered desires that once ruled us and still retain their roots very deep down in the unconscious, though all the luxuriant upper foliage has long been cut away and destroyed. It afflicts those with naturally strong passions, those in whom joy, hope, fear and grief have gone on the rampage in the past. All passions must now be related directly to God and the things of God, till they flow out from there spiritualized toward what formerly was their prime area of attraction and addiction.

John of the Cross writes much of the need to control and redirect desires. The true opposite of being ruled by one's turbulent desires is being possessed by the peace of God that passes all understanding. Practicing holy indifference is part of the route to that end.

Francis de Sales had a special grace regarding this virtue. He said, "I desire very little; and the little I desire I desire very little. In fact, I have hardly any desires. And if I were to be born again, I should prefer to have none at all" (Lehodey, *Holy Abandonment*, p. 311).

The ideal is a desirelessness of peaceful indifference, and entombment finally establishes this in the heart. Whether consolingly or barrenly, the indifference signifies the death of self-interest, not an inability to care about and for others' welfare. It is a strange fact of our relationship with God that he often gives us what we once desired after we have ceased to desire or hope for it. That is when we can accept it peacefully as his will for us instead of grabbing it as the fulfillment of what we so ardently wanted to satisfy our own need.

To be indifferent as to whether one is in a condition of entombment or resurrected new life is the ideal, for this indicates total abandonment and willingness to wait patiently for God to choose the right time. The proof that it is holy indifference lies not in any feelings, or absence of them, but in whether we continue faithfully to carry out God's will in the state of life which is ours, to adhere quietly to the pattern of prayer and receiving the sacraments that we've established long ago, and to practice abandonment as far as we are able.

It is important to remember the existence of those continuous but imperceptible direct acts hidden deep down in the crucified heart which seems to be feeling and accomplishing nothing in its deadness.

"Does God not see such desires? And do not all desires, deeply hidden though they be, speak more eloquently to God than all your words? Most certainly, such desires are acts—the best of all acts. For if you were allowed to practise self-abandonment consciously, you would find consolation once more. Yet you would lose, at least in part, the salutary perception of your wretchedness, while you would be exposed anew to the unremarked return of self-love and its disastrous complacency. You are in far greater safety at the bottom of the abyss of pure faith. Live there in peace, and await the Lord. Such peaceable and humble expectancy must keep you in a state of recollection and be counted to you for prayer" (Caussade, *Self-abandonment to Divine Providence*, p. 428).

6) *Darkness*. Whatever the previous darknesses of the dark night, none was as absolute as this of the entombment. Those who go down into the tomb alive suffer a special kind of torture of sense deprivation.

In our days torture of political dissidents has been scientifically refined into a diabolic art. It has been found that the kind of torture likely to break even the most strong-willed prisoner is to shut him up alone in a small cell with total sense deprivation—no sound, light, companionship, way of knowing the time, or whether it is night or day, or whether he has been there two days or two months. This total darkness, silence and isolation disorientate the whole being, and can end in madness.

The present day prisoner's isolation cell is a good analogy for spiritual entombment and mystical death. There is this penetrating sense of loneliness and alienation, of disturbance of the sensory apparatus, of incipient insanity, of the threat of never being able to communicate adequately again with one's own kind.

These are all symptoms of dying on one level in order to be reborn on another, the process taking place at such a profound level that it is in total darkness and silence, as it would be if buried deep down in the earth or in a bottomless cleft in perma-ice.

Yet it is in this very darkness that we encounter God in his essence, for "clouds and darkness are about his face," and his glory is such that our senses are incapable of registering it. It appears to our dazzled recording apparatus as blinding darkness.

In the tomb we are very close to God. Jesus is God, and he is lying there dead on the cold slab with us. Incorporated into him, we experience the totality of his stygian experience. It blinds us because we cannot comprehend it. Only the Spirit can comprehend the things of God, and in the tomb the spirit, though with God in us, chooses to remain an unregistered guest, as it were.

She is there, and yet not there—there in our soul, but not in our senses. The recording apparatus of our spirit is not yet fine-tuned enough to indicate where she is and what she is doing, though her activity is truly having its effect in the daily, hourly perfecting in us of abandonment to divine providence.

In *Dark Night* II,XVI, John of the Cross details "how, though in darkness, the soul walks securely." The effects of the darkness that he gives are these: There is no natural light, but this is so the soul will be illumined by supernatural light; it cannot feel; the affections have no support; the imagination cannot reflect; the memory is gone; the understanding is darkened; the will is arid; all the faculties are void and useless; it is enveloped in a cloud of affliction; it experiences itself as far from God.

The greater the darkness, the greater the security, because the faculties through which desires and temptations normally enter are all hampered or dried up—"quenched" is the word John uses. In their dark inactivity the soul is secure from vainglory, pride, presumption, vain and false rejoicing, mostly because it is rendered incapable of response, just as a paralytic cannot respond to stimuli.

In the darkness, which is contemplation, God is guiding the soul by way of the unknown to an unknown end where no natural light or faculties would be of any use. On the way there they would do nothing but hamper the soul, so they are snuffed out by grace like a candle.

"When the soul is making most progress, it is travelling in darkness, knowing naught. Therefore, since God is the Master and Guide of this blind soul, it may well and truly rejoice, once it has learned to understand this, and say: 'In darkness and secure'" (*D.N.* II,XVI,8).

The blacker the darkness, the closer to God, and the more conscious is the soul of its blindness and weakness. These are blessings because they force it to rely on God and his grace rather than on its own natural abilities and cleverness. Only in darkness is the soul able to "be secure from the enemies who inhabit (its) own house—that is, its senses and faculties" (*D.N.* II,XVI,12).

The chief characteristics of a soul immersed in this contemplative darkness are its very deep resolve to avoid all sin, to be there to do and to suffer whatever God wishes, and to follow his will and guidance in everything. Its conscience is most delicately sensitive and responsive to all the promptings of grace.

"For here all the desires and energies and faculties of the soul are recollected from all things else, and its effort and strength are employed in pleasing its God alone. After this manner the soul goes forth from itself and from all created things to the sweet and delectable union of love of God, 'in darkness and secure'" (*D.N.* II,XVI,14).

7) *Temptations.* There will be temptations in the tomb and they are almost sure to be against self-abandonment and, because of the state of exhausted quiescence, are likely to be subtle. As the soul is already in an advanced state of abandonment, they are all the more dangerous to its union with the Trinity and future progress.

Just as a small act of pure love made by a soul in this state is of immense potency for the life of the church, so is a small but deliberate fault more serious than a gross, deliberate sin in a habitual sinner. Therefore the devil tries his hardest to gain entry into the tomb of the crucified heart. He will capitalize on weaknesses already there if he can, and above all on those that damage or hinder self-abandonment. Often it is from the inherent instability natural to human beings that the temptation arises rather than directly from Satan.

There is the temptation to discontent. After all, we have little to feel content about in this state—that is, if we are able to feel at all. There are unlikely to be any consolations except of the most refined, spiritual kind that never reach the emotions or even the consciousness. It is easy to think oneself into self-pity. It may be very low key and intermittent, but it is a flaw in perfect abandonment which unquestioningly accepts from God's hand whatever he sends and does not let itself desire anything else. Without desire for something different from or extra to what one has, there would be no discontent.

There is the temptation to try to return to an earlier kind of prayer in which there were sensible consolations and plenty of "experiences" that made themselves evident.

Caussade, John of the Cross and Francis de Sales are all adamant that such a temptation must be resisted at all costs. Anyway, an attempt of this kind is almost sure to end in failure, for the recording apparatus for such events is no longer functional. You cannot run a nuclear-powered ship on coal.

There may be minor disturbances from the Inward Child (or her companions) trying to reassert herself. At this stage she is peacefully asleep in the Father's arms, but she may stir and try to get some of the attention and power to stir up trouble that she formerly had. She must be quietly shushed back to sleep and never, but never, taken out of the Father's arms into our own all-too-human ones again. She belongs to the past. We must resist her attempts to impinge on the here and now.

There is the attempt to give way to the extravagant griefs and outcries of an earlier stage. These too must be hushed. The time for drama is over. All the torments and agonies of the passion and crucifixion are behind us. There is deep suffering here in the tomb, but it is muted and must stay so, or we shall blot out the contemplative awareness growing almost imperceptibly in our stillness and abandonment.

There is the temptation to immerse oneself in distractions, comforts and human companionship. It is good to gain temporary ease through healthy enjoyments but not to seek oblivion in them. That would be like getting drunk and again would delay God's work in us and perhaps revive our taste for worldly things long renounced. It is necessary to be able to say finally to oneself, "That's enough," and return to the corpse-like abandonment and lack of distractions of the tomb.

There is the temptation to indulge in useless self-examination and in attempts to ferret out the whys and wherefores of one's state and analyze it ad nauseam. A certain amount of detached, honest self-examination and observation is salutary in revealing motives, hidden desires and manipulative processes. The danger is in the kind of introspection that makes us feel sorry for ourselves, or leads to complacency or vainglory, or that fosters negative thoughts and feelings, or that preoccupies us with ourselves instead of with God and what he wants of us and the glory and praise and thanks due to him.

Entombment and its loneliness and aridity cannot help but force us in upon ourselves. Some healthy recreation, creative activity, fresh air and exercise, laughter with friends—these ease the sense of isolation and help one not to give in to the temptation to brood.

There is the temptation to impatience. Normally God works slowly but surely—if deviously at times. We are likely to have to endure entombment for some years. It is a good idea to reconcile ourselves to this thought and to settle down to making the best of a situation that, admittedly, does not have a great deal to offer by way of either distraction or compensation.

Impatience hinders abandonment, interferes with God's action, tries to change the passivity he has chosen for us into an activity we have chosen for ourselves, and generally disturbs the peculiar peace of the tomb which, if we let ourselves, we shall start to savor after a while.

Impatience wants our own way, not God's. In the tomb, in the extremes of passivity, we must leave all initiatives to him, regarding ourselves merely as one of the pieces on the chess board that it is his right, in his wisdom, to move wherever he wants, or merely disregard.

To vary the metaphor, and move from chilliness to heat—it is like a meal cooking in a casserole. The principle is long, slow cooking at a low heat, and don't lift the lid. If the cook is impatient and keeps turning up the heat, opening the oven, lifting the lid and poking around among the ingredients, the end product will be damaged.

The secret is to put it in the oven, leave it alone, go away and do something else.

The inevitable conclusion of the entombment experience is resurrection, in the next life if not in this. Just as Jesus called, "Lazarus, come forth!" and Lazarus came, though dead and entombed for four days, so he will call each of us by name, when it is the right time for us, and we too shall emerge into the new life—either before or after death.

"The thing that is sown is perishable, but what is raised is imperishable; the thing that is sown is contemptible, but what is raised is glorious; the thing that is sown is weak, but what is raised is powerful; when it is sown it embodies the soul, when it is raised, it embodies the spirit" (1 Cor 15:42-44).

Resurrection Morning

Will resurrection morning come? Grave cloths
and spices veil that mutilated flesh
Love made into a man for us. Conspiring darkness
of this stony sepulchre curves a sheltering vault
about the corpse of God.
                                        Night-silent are all birds
and winds make no sound, waiting. Rocks
are massive sentinels honey-combed with tombs.
The guards lean on their spears, mistrustful in the mute
uncanny vigilance of this garden for the dead.

    Out of the night I cry unto thee, O Lord,
        and in the hollow sound shell of my everlasting tomb
        I raise my death-stopped voice and sing
        the canticle of the grave, the song of annihilation.

Will resurrection morning come? Who could have thought
such kingly limbs could lie so still! O long
this vigil to the dawn! World that Word spoke
strains for the lilt of his stricken tongue,
yearns, shocked, for the press of his unstirring foot.
No night songster lifts its beak. No moon gleams.
Darkness over the face of the earth. . . . The brooding night
envelops those that slew and those that mourn the slain.
Magdalen lies down in the tent of her hair, and weeps.

    Out of the night I cry unto thee, O Lord!
    In the black, bitter salt shrubs of the desert,
    in the cruel eclipse, in the hollow pit of emptiness,
    I will wait for thee, Lord, as thou commandest me.

Will resurrection morning come? Who stirs in the womb-heavy
    dimness?
(The root in the deep dungeons of the soil,
the sap in the trunk's secret tunnels, the seed
swelling to life in the grave of last year's mold.)
Death where is your sting?
                                        Light levels the dark
like a warrior's shaft. The soldiers swoon with fear
as the indomitable Word speaks the universe once more.
        In the sleeping land
a gray dawn lips the rim of the world and turns to gold.
Sorrow lasts but a night, and joy has come with the sun.

    Out of the night I cry unto thee, O lord!
    The terror of the grave surrounds me with dread—
    but thou art my help in time of trouble, my rock;
    my soul waits patiently for thy perpetual light.

18 Risen in the Lord: Emergence and Freedom

IT IS ONE of the paradoxes of our life as Christians that with baptism we are incorporated into the risen life of Christ, and yet we do not enter it in all the fullness possible until we have been purified through years of struggle and suffering, culminating in purgatory. At least, this is the usual pattern.

The new life of grace, the holiness within that flows from loving union with Jesus in all his mysteries, and especially in his passion, death, entombment and resurrection, flowers into full perfection only when the Spirit ordains. Leading up to this there will have been a continuous cycle of deaths and rebirths as grace worked within us.

Christ, as representative man and second Adam, cries out until the end of time in his continuous passion taking place in us. But he also walks the earth in us, rejoicing and exultant in his resurrection, gathering us all up into himself to witness to both realities and to renew all things in and through him, since we are custodians of this world.

"By the same power with which he can subdue the whole universe" the risen Lord "will transfigure these wretched bodies [and souls] of ours into copies of his glorious body [and soul]" (Phil 3:21). Our transfiguration will extend itself into the world about us, and above all, into the social order and our relationships with others.

"Christ's redemptive work, while of itself directed toward the salvation of men, involves also the renewal of the whole temporal order. Hence the mission of the Church is not only to bring to men the message and grace of Christ, but also to penetrate and perfect the temporal sphere with the spirit of the gospel" (*Decree on the Apostolate of the Laity*, 5).

The spirit of the gospel is essentially the life-giving message, he

181

is risen! Let us rejoice! When at last the stone is rolled away from the tomb doorway, and Jesus rises in us and comes forth into the world, what can we expect?

In the first place, it is unwise to "expect" anything, for the resurrection will be personalized in us by the Spirit. Infinite Wisdom will choose when and how the risen Lord is to manifest himself through us, and until it happens, we can have no accurate idea of how it will be. But one thing is sure, there will be a profound realization that he has risen in us for others and wishes to use us in servanthood to them. We have probably already been apostles in one way or another, but now in a more intimate, all-encompassing manner we are to be used as never before.

Love is service. Now that perfect Love has true freedom to be at work in and through us, he will require of us a vocation of total self-giving for others in some way that he will choose for us. At the Last Supper he had said to the Father, "Glorify your Son so that your Son may glorify you. . . . Let him give eternal life to all those you have entrusted to him. . . . I have glorified you on earth and finished the work that you gave me to do . . . As you sent me into the world, I have sent them into the world" (Jn 17:1-4, 18).

Jesus risen has given us his glory and eternal life so that we can pass them on to others. He is sending us out to impregnate the world with this new life. We are to be his servants, messengers, channels, repositories, proclaimers and reckless dispensers of divine love. Our agony, mystical death and resurrection were to bring us to the state where the Lord could take each of us, as a tool, into his right hand and say, "Here is just the perfect instrument I've been seeking for that special work that needs doing. I shall use it for that."

Teresa of Avila wrote, "Do you know when people really become spiritual? It is when they become the slaves of God and are branded with his sign, in token that they have given him their freedom. Then he can sell them as slaves to the whole world as he himself was sold" (*Mansions* Vii,v).

What are the signs that the Lord has risen in a soul and life, that a person is ready for the apostolate wisdom has chosen for him, that Love has been poured into her and the channel cleared for it to pour out to others, that she has emerged from the constricting darkness of death and the tomb into the light and freedom of full union with the divine will?

Those indicated below exclude all extraordinary manifestations of divine invasion for these are, by themselves, no true indication of holiness or even of mission.

Emergence

In some form or other we shall have a sense of change, coming forth, easing of inner darkness into light, being born again.

This may be quite a dramatic and almost instantaneous interior change, probably consisting in an awareness of emergence from darkness to light; a strange, compelling sense of saying with Jesus, "It is finished"; silence within the grinding machinery of decades-long suffering, stress and struggle suddenly cease; a penetrating peace that takes over and persists; the fading away of all images of anguish, torture, deprivation, loneliness, and their replacement by a certainty, solid yet indefinable, that Someone is there and will never depart, or seem to, again; a lyrical burst of joy like the first day of spring, that may lessen in intensity but remains in sharp contrast to our former agony; a prosaic certainty that the casserole (to use an earlier image) has been taken from the oven, the lid lifted, the contents investigated and pronounced ready for eating, and the meal begun.

On the other hand, the emergence may occur in fits and starts over a longer or shorter period, almost as if the stone was rolled away a few inches, we peeped out, saw the stars, sniffed the fresh, delicious air, then were dragged back as the aperture closed and an implacable voice said, "Not yet. You aren't quite ready. Get back on the grave slab again. I'll call you later on."

This to and fro procedure may go on for as long as it takes us to reach the stage of holy indifference as to whether it happens, does not happen, releases us finally, or confines us finally. It may lengthen its cycles so we actually come out to taste the dawn in the garden, walk about, utter prayers of praise and thanksgiving for release, and then are put back, without explanation, into dark incarceration again.

The Spirit uses his own techniques to suit what he knows we need. Whichever way it happens, emergence has its own special flavor of freedom.

Freedom

The glorious liberty of the sons and daughters of God is the

Trinity's resurrection gift to us. "We are the children, not of the slave-girl, [Hagar], but of the free-born wife, [Sarah]" (Gal 4:31).

We were not born into this world to be slaves but heirs with Christ to the kingdom of heaven within, everything at our disposal, with all the privileges that go with this state. Our lives till now have been more or less imprisoned in the first syndrome, or else struggling in the second to free ourselves. Now we are like the monarch butterfly at last completely out of the chrysalis and ready to fly, our wings dry, taut and outspread to sail freely in the light-joy-fulfillment syndrome.

St. Teresa, in writing of the prayer of union (*Mansions* V,ii), uses the analogy of the silkworm. The soul, she tells us, is like the silkworm which spins itself a chrysalis after it has become full-grown through its feeding on the food for holiness and remedies for sin provided by the church.

In John of the Cross' terms, the soul has done all it can in the active nights to do God's will, eliminate any deliberate sin, practice virtue and love God and neighbor.

The chrysalis it spins is the house in which it is to die and this house is Christ, for our life is hidden away in Christ, and we were baptized into him. We work as hard as we can at making our cocoon of virtue, and God adds his gift of Jesus himself to our efforts.

Teresa writes, "Let us renounce our self-love and self-will and our attachment to earthly things. . . . Let the silkworm die—let it die, as in fact it does when it has completed the work which it was created to do" (*Mansions* V,ii). (Its death and change hidden in the chrysalis is the equivalent of the night of faith, the onset of contemplation, and the initial passive purgations.)

From the silkworm's death emerges the butterfly, image of the state of union of the human will with God's will. Teresa is here speaking of a lesser state of union than that of full spiritual marriage, but what she says is relevant to both states and especially of the soul freed from entombment. "That soul has now delivered itself into (God's) hands and his great love has so completely subdued it that it neither knows nor desires anything save that God shall do with it what he wills. Never, I think, will God grant this favour save to the soul which he takes for his very own. His will is that, without understanding how, the soul shall go thence sealed with his seal" (*Mansions* V,ii).

Those who are freed from the tomb are indelibly branded with the cross as Christ's forever. Just as the cross was Jesus' route to freedom, so has it been for them.

Paradoxically, the glorious liberty begins when the human will becomes fused with God's and never claims autonomy again, even though involuntary failures to concur perfectly remain. It increases as self-abandonment to divine providence gradually takes over until we experience it according to those various images of passivity in abandonment that were detailed earlier.

To lie in God's will like driftwood in a current of water is to be free as human beings were created to be free. God made us for himself. Human fulfillment in its highest form is to be one with God. Being one with God means having one's will inseparably mingled with his as water poured from one vessel into another also containing water becomes indistinguishably one with it.

We are then free because we have become what it is our nature to be. To be completely fulfilled is to be utterly free. The butterfly, emerged from the chrysalis, is now free to live out what was inbuilt into the tiny egg from which the silkworm first hatched. It has reached the apogee of its existence—flight in the air. This is the equivalent of the soul's love-flight in the Spirit, that immense inner uplifting into grace, love and wholeness sometimes expressed through the body in levitation.

God's will for us is the upwelling of his love within us, adapted to the uniqueness of each separate person. Freedom means being wide open to receive that love, all barriers and defenses down, all ifs, buts, whys and hows silenced, all sorrow and resentment at not getting what we thought we wanted and were entitled to stilled. His love will inundate us to the exact degree that we are open to receive it. Freedom from entombment means our aperture of receptivity is as fully dilated as God intended when he brought us into being.

From now on we drink in all the graces he offers us, refusing nothing, everything absorbed and becoming the food on which the holiness he has implanted in us will grow. There is nothing to hinder his work of continuously bringing us closer and closer to that level of perfection that he wills for us. This will come about at the moment of our death, and then we shall pass immediately into face-to-face encounter with him.

The fullest freedom is the freedom to attain this degree of union. Until we emerge from the entombment, we are hampered by all the elements of self-love, self-will and self-interest within ourselves detailed in earlier chapters. After we emerge we are freed from their power over us. They are either dead, comatose or so quelled by grace that they are impotent to hinder our receptivity to God's will and life and our response to his love.

We are now free to love others with a love uncontaminated by self-seeking. Our love is limpid, simple, pure, unconditional, cleansed of manipulation and emotionalism. We need not fear to love, for whatever we feel is Spirit-infused and full of the joy of the Lord instead of provoked by hidden needs and hungers over which we once endlessly rationalized.

It follows that we are free of all emotional entanglements. It has become impossible for us to enter into them, for we are not dependent upon any human being for emotional sustenance. Being fed spiritually all the time by God means a fulfillment so far transcending that of the natural emotions, for which we once craved, that to return to it would be like throwing away an open check that can draw on absolutely unlimited riches to grasp at one for a hundred dollars.

We are free from being ruled by the four passions of joy, hope, fear and grief. At last they are spiritualized and directed toward God and the things of God. It is the Spirit who arouses them in us, not our own earthy needs, desires, addictions and anxieties.

Our freedom has come largely through the development of our self-abandonment from acceptance of, submission to, and waiting upon God's will, to an active love of it that subsumes all previous reactions.

This active, positive love of the divine will, however and whenever it represents itself to us, brings freedom from joy only when that will goes our way and satisfies our cravings, from hope to have in the future the satisfactions it has not yet brought us, from fear it will take from us what we have and want to keep, from grief when it has already deprived us.

Freed from the often wild oscillations caused by being tossed about by these passions, we are now able to rest undisturbed and constantly in the sacrament of the present moment. Whatever it brings, we have become unshakably certain that this is exactly right for us where we stand and how we are here and now. We are finally and completely convinced of this, and we love his will because it so unfailingly brings us what we need, whether we are conscious of it or not, and whether or not that is what we ourselves would have chosen as apt.

We are freed of the anxiety to know God's will before it presents or reveals itself, to understand why it is operating in these particular ways, to make the right diagnosis about ourselves, or others, or God's action, to leap ahead of divine providence and do things in our own way at the times we choose. Loving his will just as it is, uncamouflaged by us, bestows all these blessings of freedom.

As a result, inner confusion and muddle are eliminated in the simplicity of unconditional love and acceptance. Lifelong obsessions and worries against which we have struggled for many years have been dissolved away. Unfinished business and grieving labor become problems of the past. Resentment, account-making, hankering after this and that, impatience for things to happen and for plans and projects to come to fruition—they all drop behind as we emerge from the tomb into freedom.

At last, loving God's will so peacefully and wholly, trusting it so unquestioningly, we are freed from wanting anything or anyone but it and him. This does not mean we cease to love others. On the contrary, for the first time we are able to love with purity of intention whoever and whatever God puts in our way. We are freed to forgive from the depths of our heart whoever has hurt and caused us previously inconsolable grief. We no longer need to judge them or anyone. Our hypersensitivity and over-reaction patterns have been blotted out as we lay in the tomb. This means we are automatically healed of the negative and baneful effects of former sufferings. Now we love our beloveds whether or not they are kind to us and love us in return. We love them for God's sake, not our own.

It is a glorious freedom to love without the humiliating need to extract love in return. The term free love takes on a whole new meaning. We no longer suffer negative reactions to the "nothing for you" message. If nothing is God's will for us at this moment, in this situation, then we bless and actively love that nothing as the most precious gift he could bestow on us. We say cheerfully to him, "OK, Father. I don't mind. Another time—or way—will do. You know best. Arrange it your way, and don't take any notice of what I say."

There is no longer need for either self-abasement or self-aggrandizement, for fear of rejection or longing for approval. We are operating freely from the still center of Spirit-bestowed self-knowledge and self-acceptance. We are who we are, in spite of all our sufferings, labors and purgations. Pitiful objects, yet glorious with the presence of the Trinity within, we have the certain promise of glory being added to glory the more we open ourselves to receive what God only waits upon our receptivity to give.

That giving comes through the sacrament of the present moment. Loving God's will as we now do, we constantly embrace and receive this sacrament of his own unsurpassable love. A warning bell sounds within us whenever we are tempted to disregard this sacrament. It reminds us of our former enslavement to our own restless desires and addictions, and we realize anew that we never want to be like that again. The last thread holding the bird tied down has broken. It is free and soaring, and we remain on guard against ever again causing its confinement.

"When Christ freed us, he meant us to remain free. Stand firm, therefore, and do not submit again to the yoke of slavery" (Gal 5:1).

Those who have emerged from the corpse-like abandonment of the tomb into the glorious liberty of the risen Lord feel as if their uttermost depths are being opened to eternity and infinity. There is a sublime interchange with God in which they are freely flowing into him through the aperture and he into them. There is not a single impediment left to come between lover and beloved. They merge together in a vast inner space without any clutter, where all is composure and simplicity and Christ walks at his ease.

A strange completion in nothingness and emptiness which is absolute fullness possesses them. There is a sense of final safety and the end of a process that will in fact never end. At the same time as it *is*, it *is yet to be*.

In the center of shimmering joy, peace, love and thanksgiving is the jewel of freedom, still and life-transmitting. Because it takes place within a human being confined in time and space and a fleshly body, this freedom and interflowing, and the awareness of it, vary in intensity. But even when arid darkness returns for a while, the deep peace remains and the grace of pure love of God's will from which the freedom originates is never taken away.

The freed will enter the fullness of transforming union when, how and to the degree divine providence decrees. Abandoned to it, they wait in peaceful expectation, aware of God's presence, and embrace it through his will operative in their lives. By their loving union with it, they are spiritually married to it. In the past they had cried out against it, or sought to modify it, because they thought they knew better. Now, all obstacles gone, they are open to receive it in all its fullness and grace.

> If anyone loves me he will keep my word,
> and my Father will love him,
> and we shall come to him
> and make our home with him. . . .
> A peace the world cannot give, this is my gift to you. . . .
> Make your home in me, as I make mine in you
> (Jn 14:23,27; 15:4).

One of the gifts that Jesus himself promised us was peace, specifically designated his peace.

There are no words to the soul's endless alleluia before the ineffable glories of the Godhead. Its song of praise has become its way of life and habitual disposition. Everything speaks to it of God and manifests his power and glory.

The promised peace of his presence is everywhere, both in the soul's own inner depths and in the universe, each equally unfathomable. Steeped in this peace, in its "inmost substance," the soul constantly experiences the reality of the divine indwelling.

No human can plumb the mysteries of deep space, and so it is in the depths of the spirit which merge with the depths of the Holy Spirit himself. Here "The Beloved dwells most secretly, with more intimate, more interior and closer embrace, according as the soul is the more purely and completely withdrawn from all save God" (*L.F.* IV,5,14).

This withdrawal has come about progressively as peace was established ever more deeply at the mental, emotional and psychological strata of the inner spaces. Now the spirit opens out to merge with the infinity that is God, in "this sweet embrace made in the depth of the substance of the soul" (L.F. IV,5,14), where, as St. John of the Cross puts it, it has fruition of its Beloved. "He is there, habitually, as it were, asleep in this embrace with the bride in the substance of the soul" (*L.F.* IV,5,15).

There are few mere powerful images of crowned and perfect Peace than this of united married lovers, profoundly sleeping in each other's arms. Even in sleep each retains an intuitive consciousness of the beloved "resting and reposing in its breast." In order to guard this precious, hard-won peace, its possessor will avoid anything or anyone that could threaten distraction or disturbance.

Those who have thus clasped the pearl of great price will defend it with their life. Unerring intuitions prompted by divine Wisdom at work in their depths will warn them where danger lies and help them fortify their inner being from its intrusion.

As they continue with the necessary business of living, they will be able to render to God what is God's, and to Caesar what is Caesar's, with perfect justice and equilibrium. They now live with their inner spaces open to eternity and infinity, with the Trinity flowing through them, in direct contact with

> God, the Father of our Lord Jesus Christ,
> who has blessed us with all the spiritual blessings of
>   heaven in Christ . . .
> to make us praise the glory of his grace,
> his free gift to us in the Beloved,
> in whom, through his blood, we gain our freedom, the
>   forgiveness of our sins (Eph 1:3, 6-7).

And so peace in the depths, established on all levels—mental, emotional, psychological and spiritual—is the sign that the kingdom of heaven is formed in the soul. From it radiates happiness and contentment that no earthly force can annihilate. All the allurements of the world have lost their power to attract or compel. The sense of liberation is so strong that the soul seems like a thistledown effortlessly afloat in the currents of the divine will in which it has perfect trust and uninterrupted fulfillment.

"There is only Christ. He is everything and he is in everything" (Col 3:11).

The New Season

Waiting is purification,
is patience quelling desire,
is God's time permeating human haste.

The crystal droplet
gathers at the curled leaf's tip
but does not fall.
The mighty wave bounds in
but does not break.

The heart's new season
pauses on the threshold
of the walled, inviolate garden,
the spring of living waters at its center.

We wait till that authoritative voice
cries once more, "Come forth!
Begin to bud and bloom!
Toss in the breezes of my ardent love!
Be all renewed and filled with light!
Waiting is over—
the hour of fulfillment come!"

Beloved, this is our new season.
Together let us go to meet it.